Soldiers Poetry

From the Regimental Museum Archives

of the

Sherwood Foresters

Arranged and Presented
By
Cliff Housley

Soldiers Poetry

From the Regimental Museum Archives
of the
Sherwood Foresters

Published by
MILIQUEST PUBLICATIONS
83, Draycott Road, Sawley,
Long Eaton, Nottingham NG10 3 BL

ISBN 0 9529648 5 6

INTRODUCTION

Over the years many donations have been made to the Regimental Museum and amongst such gifts have been personal artefacts and paperwork. Sometimes, the gifts were from the family of a deceased soldier of the regiment and on other occasions, an officer or soldier himself made the gifts.

A considerable amount of time has been taken up in the sorting and cataloguing of these hundreds of letters, notes, maps, and other papers. As a result of the detailed cataloguing it has become apparent that there is, contained within the Regimental Archives, a considerable wealth of poems or verse.

Not only is interesting information to be found within these verses, but also, there is at times, as might be expected of soldiers when at war, a considerable amount of nostalgia and sentiment.

Many of the verses condemn the situation or circumstances in which the writer found himself and in so doing, he no doubt speaks for the thousands of soldiers in any war who ever suffered similar events and circumstances.

Soldiers' poetry is by its very nature descriptive and provides a picture of either the surroundings, or of the mental mood of the writer. There is a distinct difference in the poetry of a prisoner of war or a man in hospital having been wounded, from that of his comrades who are still fighting on.

The verses in this book are then the thoughts of some of the men of The Sherwood Foresters The Nottinghamshire and Derbyshire regiment, set down on scraps of paper as and when time allowed. The poems cover The Crimean War, The Boer War, The Great War of 1914-18 and the Second World War of 1939-45, together with those written by Prisoners of war.

CH

MISS NIGHTINGALE – The Crimean War

By 3628 Private James Reynard.
(95th Derbyshire Regiment, circa 1854.)

On a dark stormy night and the Crimea's dread shore,
There was bloodshed and strife, on the morning before,
The dead and dying lay bleeding around,
Some crying for help, seemed not to be found,
Now God in his mercy, he pities their cries,
The soldier so cheerful in the morning did rise,
Singing forward, my lads, let your hearts never fail,
You are cheered by the presence of Miss Nightingale.

Now, God sent this woman to succour the brave,
Thousands she has saved, from an untimely grave,
Her eyes beam with pleasure, she is so busy and good,
The wants by the wounded, are by her understood,
With fever, some was brought in, their lives almost gone,
Others with disable limbs, broken badly, and torn,
Keep up your spirits lads, let you heart never fail,
You are cheered by the help of sweet Nightingale.

Her heart, it means good, no bounty she takes,
She would lay down her life for a poor soldiers sake,
She prays for the dying, gives peace to the brave,
She knows that a soldier has a soul for to save,
The wounded, they love her, it can be seen,
She is the soldier's preserver, they call her their Queen,
May God give her strength, let her heart never fail,
One of Heavens best gifts was sweet Florence Nightingale.
The wives of the wounded, how thankful they are,
Their husbands are cared for, and attention is paid,
Whatever the country, this gift God has given,
The soldiers they say she is an angel from Heaven,
Sing praise to this woman, deny it who can,
All women were sent here for the comfort of Man,
I hope no more against them, you'll rail,
Treat them well and may they prove to be like,
Sweet Florence Nightingale.

Hospital Tents Balaclava Ridge 1955

THE VOLUNTEERS SONG

I am a Rifle Volunteer,
And quite particular to rules;
Ner march, nor drill, howe'er severe,
My military ardour cools;
I arm but in my country's cause,
To keep her from the Eagles' claws;
If they attempt a swoop to make,
Crack! Crack! My course is clear;
They'll find they've made a slight mistake-
I am a Volunteer!

I am a Rifle Volunteer,
And they who are not so, are mules!
My nerve is firm, my sight is clear,
For exercise, digestion schools.
My pluck is good, upon parade,
To face the wet, I'm ne'er afraid;
And should the foemen dare invade,
Crack! Crack! My shot, they'll hear,
My country and my Queen to aid-
I am a Volunteer!

Unsigned, newspaper article found in Robin Hood Rifles album P112 in Regimental Archives.

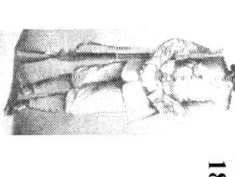

(Robin Hood Rifles, circa 1860.)

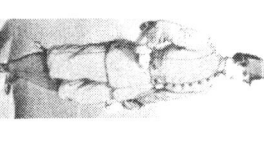

ON THE PRESENTATION OF COLOURS TO THE RIBIN HOOD BY THE LADIES OF NOTTINGHAM

Unfurl the banners-let them wave,
Above the gallant and the free;
Ne'er must the coward of the slave,
Beneath their shadow shelter'd be.

All unstain'd now, their silken sheen;
But, though no name renown'd in story,
Glitters upon the Lincoln Green,
And stamps at once its warlike glory.

Should note of war, from foreign land,
Be wafted o'er the Channel wave,
We know that yonder noble band,
Is ready Throne and Realm to save.

For hearth and home we boldly ask,
Of them protection from the foe;
Be ours the sweet and holy task,
To share their joy, and smile away their woe.

Signed L.S.T., dated Oct.3rd 1860. Newspaper article, found in Robin Hood Rifles album P112 in Regimental Archives. (Robin Hood Rifles, circa 1860.)

How dare snobs, who never,
Mustered round mess tables,
Do "guards", "rounds", "inspections",
"rooms", "parades" or "stables"?
How dare they, who scarce know,
What "Eyes right!" or "Dress!" is,
Poke their noses into Military messes?

Unsigned, newspaper article, found in Robin Hood Rifles album P112 in Regimental Archives. (Robin Hoods circa 1860)

CONFOUND THEIR IMPUDENCE

Volunteer cads- hang them!
Dare to grumble- hang them!
When we, of the Service,
Condescend to slang them!
Plead, that in a field day,
Or review, no wonder,
Amateurs, or regulars,
Should commit a blunder.

Hint at how at Wormwood Scrubs,
And Aldershot too,
Line and Guards don't always
Know where they have got to.
That there have been cases,
Of what we call "clubbing",
District Generals "wigging",
Even Horse-Guards "snubbing".

That a Brigadier,
Not a very bright one,
Has been known to give the
Wrong word for the right one.
That, if Volunteers,
Do sometimes make muddles,
Blaze away their bayonets,
Or get into huddles.

Are long closing into square,
Or opening out of it,
Will talk in the ranks,
Or turn heads, not a doubt of it.
'Twasn't Volunteers,
But regular Queen's shillings,
Set Dragoon Guards riding,
Into Inniskillings.

VICTORIA'S MIDDAY REVIEW

They tell us a tale that we dare not ignore;
That deep in a glade we have hunted before,
A tiger's waiting to spring,
And so we come up to our Queen,
As of yore, our fathers came up to their King.

The beast that is lurking is fiercer, they say,
Than the tiger our fathers brought grimly to bay,
And rolled in his blood at their feet.
And therefore we come to our Lady today,
The vow of our sires to repeat.

We come with firm footstep, as hunters should tread,
With the glaive by the side, with the plume on the head,
With the heart where a hunter's should be;
And each with the weapon of weapons most dread,
Most dread, in the hands of the Free.

Nor idly we come in a holiday pride,
With arms unaccustomed, with sinews untried,
To deal with a savage so fell;
We know from our sires, when a savage hath died,
His hunter's have quit them right well.

And we come that the Lady of Kingdoms may know,
In the day, should it chance, that her bugles shall blow,
She shall find Hunter-Soldiers astir;
And the men whom her signal shall launch on the foe,
Shall be worthy of dying for her.

From the loom, from the mine, from the forge, from the mart,
From the cells of stern science, the halls of fair art,
From the homes of calm Learning, we come;
And some that he is but s monster to fright,
Who grudges his brother a brotherly part,
In our work-let him hence, and be dumb!

Some say the War-Tiger is scared from the fight;
And some that his courage hath quailed to a blight,
From the scent of our fresh flowing sea;
And some that he is but s monster to fright,
The folks near his home. It may be.

But our fields they lie open, our gardens are rare,
And those we love better than life, wander there,
And our babies are crawling about,
And none of us all is so brave as to dare,
To leave certain questions in doubt.

We come, but it is not in plaint or in fear,
Which, did the Queen, proudly marking us hear,
In the voice of that thunder-toned shout.
We've come but to show her what hunters are near,
For the hour when her bugles ring out.

So we come in our thousands, from cot and from hall,
And from thousands again who are ready at call,
Should o11ce the War-Tiger be seen,
And this is the errand on which, one and all,
We come up today, to the Queen.

Did they daunt the brave hunters in years have gone by,
That foam on his fangs, and that fire in his eye,
As he rushed in his rage on the spear?
No, thus, ever thus, the War-Tiger should die:
Come Tiger, the Hunters are here.

The blood-thirsty growl and the roar are in vain;
If the savage attack us, the savage again,
Shall wr the in a merited doom;
There's the steel for his flank, and the ball for his brain,
Come, Tiger, and spring on thy tomb.

Unsigned, newspaper article, found in Robin Hood Rifles album P112 in Regimental Archives. (circa 1860)

"BEFORE MAGDALA." (13th april 1868.)

It chanced that morning
When every warning,
Had failed to make Theodore chuck up,
That the King, he lay drunk,
And so shook with funk,
That he couldn't speak, but hiccup.

While he thought on the bones
Of the slaughter'd ones
Lying starkly and rigidly stiff.
Whom with blood on his breath,
He had doom'd to death,
Or had dash'd down the Magdala cliff.

There by Fahla's height,
In the early light,
Were the Sherwood woodmen biding.
The time to go,
In at the foe,
And give them a proper hiding.

The Officers squatted,
So as not be potted,
While Furnemore made a new will
Made Lieutenant D.T.
His sole legatee,
And sent him the key of the till.

And Beamish thought,
Of commissions bought,
That the tin might be lost to his people,
Hummed the battle air
*And of the puritan pair
And gazed up at Magdala Steeple.

And the Count did think,
Could he get but a drink,
He would stump up all his dollars.
Scatter "Kentish fires"
Through Tory Shires
And exist in turn-down collars.

And in ravenous mood,
From the elephant's food,
Sabin Gogo would snatch a big bite.
And in onions and honey,
Would spend all his money
The chrysalis-warrior Wright.

And Adjutant Jack Gage,
He made up a package,
Addressed to D.T. at Ashangi,
Inside was a lock,
From the tuft of a cock,
For the cock hat of the new S.M.G.

And close he did gnaw,
Some beef, nearly raw,
While rowing, such stuff he never eat.
Fast then slipt by,
Close under his eye, A sleek Abyssinian leveret.

Then close he did say,
In a nonchalant way,
"It's all bosh what care I for a brevet?"
And of Major, the style,
With starvation meanwhile,
Tut: give me a peg and a leveret.

And Mrs.Reeve,
She did sigh for leave,
To fall out and follow the beast.
Though she daily had dollops
Of fat mutton collops,
At the Quarter Masters feast.

And Beamish and they,
Well nigh every day,
When the rest of the army was starving,
Had of rations full quota,
Hazrees, burra and chota,
So the question was who should do the carving?

Kidneys and liver,
And whatso' iver,
Was laid by for them by the butchers,
Lights and sweet bread!
'Twas on such they fed!
And cold tiffin sent on by the cutchas.

Now just as the sound
Of a hoof on the ground,
Announced Major General Staveley,
Jack Preston caught
Such a merry thought,

That with drum sticks he'd fight bravely!
Oh! A chicken I see!
Who'll catch it myself I suppose.
I must catch it myself I suppose.
Jack Gage the wink tip,
Give the Colonel the slip,
For I'm that peckish, nobody knows.

For without any rum,
Or the cheering drum,
For the musick was given to G's wing,
And without even port,
Of the hospital sort,
As Furnemore's chary of beeswing.

I've trudged many a mile,
In the very best style,
And now that we're in for an action,
I say it, who shouldn't,
(In my case, who wouldn't),
Think a bellyful, greater attraction?

So after that hen,
To her innermost den,
If it's all up the Magdala heights,
I'll pursue and will catch,
And will eat, and dispatch,
To the Colonel, the liver and lights.

So Preston, he went,
On a spatch cock intent,
And made a great rush at the chicken.
While the 33rd stormed,
And the 45th formed,
For to give Theodorus a licken.

Then just as Jack Preston,
Did think he possess'd one,
Lo! Into a hut, she skedaddled!
And all he did get,
Was a great deal of sweat,
And he picked up an egg that was addled.

Then determined to win,
He followed it in,
And instantly found himself collar'd,
And raged in vain,
Like a king of Spain,
As portrayed by Augustus Pollard!

And the hut was dark,
And a dog did bark,
While the fowl made a terrible clatter.
Then out stumped Jack,
With a thing on his back,
So the army cried, "What's the matter?"

BATTLE BEFORE MAGDALA, ABYSSINIA, APRIL 13TH 1868

Then as Jack drew near,
"Well", they said it's queer!
There's something adrift with the skipper.
And sure he began,
To strike out like a man,
But in vain, he tried to pip her!

And so, in the dearth,
Of all food for mirth,
They all shrieked, "Look at Preston's bag"!
For instead of a hen,
He'd got hold of the wen,
Of a sexegenarian hag!

Then the stormers stopp'd,
And their rifles dropped,
The army roared with laughter.
Screamed fiddle-dee-dee,
To the C. in C.
When he said, "What on earth are they after."

Then the King look'd down,
Through a spout in the town,
And thought, "What can they be, artur?"
His General's said,
We see Preston's head,
Said the King, "And he's caught a tarter!"

Such squeaking and squalling,
Head over ears falling!
Oh! Such a kicking and spluttering!
Jack as pale as death,
And under his breath,
Some County Cork adjectives muttering!

While the old 'un gave tongue,
And leech-like she clung,
Much fearing she went to the slaughter,
And then you might see,
On the skipper's coatee,
There was much perspiration and water.

Then Hayward he cried,
As he ran to her side,
Tayib! Old girl, here's your Hayward!
But she only reeched,
Beseeched and screeched,
And was mafisch and most wayward.

Then Staveley, he cried,
That she that did ride,
Was an old Abyssinian lady,
Who had taken Jack,
For an Irish hack,
Since his coat was somewhat shady.

Take her down tenderly,
Fashioned so slenderly,
Have a care, see those poor lips of her,
Oozing so clammily,
One of Eve's family,
How could you let that hen slip, Sir?

So they took her down,
By Magdala town,
But the breath had left her body,
And never did Jack,
Feel more the lack,
Of a peg of whisky toddy.

And they who cried,
That saw her ride,
She'll come to a queer end, oh!
The same they said,
When she was dead,
De lunatico inquirendo.

Then they stormed the cliff,
Which was very stiff,
And Jack wobbled in, a victor.
But the people said,
If we'd not fled,
You'd never dare have kick'd her!

And the King lay dead,
With a hole in his head,
But they saved young Alamayo,
And the Royal slip,
Did then take ship,
And is now with the Earl of Mayo.

*Duet from Opera I Puritani.

Postscript Madras

And you'll find any day,
Should you come this way,
The Count tete-a-tete with old Higgins,
Or likely enough,
His Elizabethan ruff,
He'll be settling on in his diggings.

And di Thoren was sold,
Of Finnermore's gold,
For the latter's in excellent trim,
Drives every day,
With Marshal hey,
Who's cuts with General Prim.

And of Beamish enquire,
What he did under fire,
When he marched on the Magdala steeple?
You'll be friends for life,
If you tell him the strife,
Was worthy of him and his people!

And when some have talk'd,
That the wing was baulk'd,
Of the glory – and he got no roughing,
It's all fiddle-dee-dee!
Go ask Hooke or D.T!
Or be plucky and ask the Puffin!

"And forever and forever,
As long as the river's flow,
As long as the heart hath passions,
As long as life hath woe."

The story of Captain Preston,
And the black hag on his back,
Will be told by countless Foresters,
In memory of Jack!

General Horace Lockwood, Smith-Dorrien, (D.S.O.) writing on events of 13th April 1868.

FAIRFIELD COMMON, Buxton, Derbyshire
(Encampment of the 3rd Battn. of Derbyshire
Militia, Chatsworth Rifles, Under the Command of
Col. Lord Edward Cavendish, M.P., June 1886.)

Here we are on Fairfield Common,
Come to take our annual drills,
And mingle with rich men and women,
Who seek a change for worldly ills.

We "stand at ease", prompt at "attention",
And "shoulder arms" at the command;
And "port" or "slope", or aught you mention.
"Presenting arms" as we pass the grand.

The charm of music melts to tears,
Or maddens blood, too soon on fire;
Whilst the martial tread of Volunteers,
Is what the Officers so much admire.

We "mount the guard" each in his turn,
And pickets send both up and down;
And little have we cause to mourn,
As stragglers we pick up from town.

Snug in our tents, on beds long feathered,
We take our rest after each day's work,
And sleep quite soundly, if not be-weathered,
Enjoying sundry hours of talk.

With camp fires lit and kettles boiling,
As sentinels pace each well trod beat;
The bugle sounds, to breakfast calling,
For those with appetites to eat.

When drill is over off we go,
Rambling over hill and dale;
And note the wild flowers, how they grow,
In Ashwoods rock-bound lovely vale.

Some roam away as they get leave,
To Wormhill village in the Peak;
Others confiding friends but grieve,
In gaining hearts to leave and break.

To Peak Forest Village, or Dove Holes,
A pleasant stroll it is to some;
Enjoying, perhaps a game at bowls,
And return to camp ere beat of drum.

To "Corbar Walks", or "Cat and Fiddle",
"Pooles's Cave", "Axe Edge", or "Lovers' Leap",
And hear the wild birds sweetly warble,
As we at these just take a peep.

From "Camp" to "Devonshire", "Bull", "Pavilion",
To hear Karl Meyder and his band,
Is it a treat indeed, for England's million,
Or the fair and lovely of our land.

Perfect in drill, and conduct too,
Is what we hope for and long may want;
While few the failures, we've yet in view,
The vote for Capitation grant.

We "march" and "counter-march", and "wheel",
As our band plays past in brilliant style,
With "bayonets fixed" with glittering steel,
By companies of each rank and file.

And ere the terms of drill expire,
A grand field day we have for you;
As rapidly our rifles fire,
Ending with a grand review.

And whilst our Officers, at mess,
Listen to their well-trained band,
Time passes pleasantly, ne'ertheless,
To those who chance outside to stand.

Ere tents are struck, a Ball is given,
To those who e'er admire the brave,
And in its mazes, dream of Heaven,
Regretting they must leave.

But should our country e'er demand,
The aid of well trained Volunteers,
We'll follow, bravely, those in command,
And meet our foes with manly cheers.

Signed J.Bates, circa 1886.
In papers of Frank Brindley, (Captain, M.C.,
2/6th Battalion)

IN MEMORIUM OF JOHNATHAN WHITE.

Joined as one man, ten thousand townsmen mourn,
O'er the cold clay of one, whose duty done,
Needing his rest-to rest is aptly borne:
And obsequies honourable, honourably won.

True British heart! True soldier and true man!
Honest old her! Whose spirit could inspire,
And ever did responsive spirit fan,
Now o'er thy grave we tribute volleys fire.

White was thy fame, as was thy honoured name,
Humble! Yet noble, modest, yet so brave!
Intrepid, cool! Fearless of aught but shame.
Tumult of war for thee no more shall rave.
Eternal peace be thine, beyond the grave.

Signed F.W., dated May 16th 1889
Newspaper article, found in Robin Hood Rifles album P112 in Regimental Archives.

Written on the death of Jonathan White.
(Major, Robin Hood Rifles, circa 1889)

A LETTER TO DEAR OLD ENGLAND

A letter to dear old England, that land so pure and fair,
What joy 'tis to a loving heart so fondly beating there,
Dear friend! I'll never forget you, wherever I may roam,
Nay, I will send them, when I can, a loving letter home.

I bid farewell to England, and dread the dangerous wave,
For thirty days upon the sea, amongst the true and brave,
We meet with adventures, upon the troubled main,
But, I will tell you all of them, when next we meet again.

I bade farewell to England, for duty calls me here,
To guard her rights in India, through every passing year,
Until a few shall pass away and time shall seem free,
Then in a while with faithful heart, I will return to thee.

I landed far from England, on India's ragged strand,
To witness many wondrous sights, in this far distant land,
We marched through dusk and darkness, and felt no fear not toil,
For we are British soldiers, and can bear it with a smile.

Oft now when far from England, strange thoughts pass through my mind,
Of pleasure, hope, and love, and joy, which make me turn and smile;
I miss those happy voices in this far distant land,
But may I soon return again to join them hand.

Tell my friends in England I left so true and kind,
Tell them I never shall forget the friends I left behind,
I wish them health and happiness, wherever they may be,
May God for ever bless them, and keep old England free.

Signed Private G.M.
(Private, 2nd Battalion c.1890's)

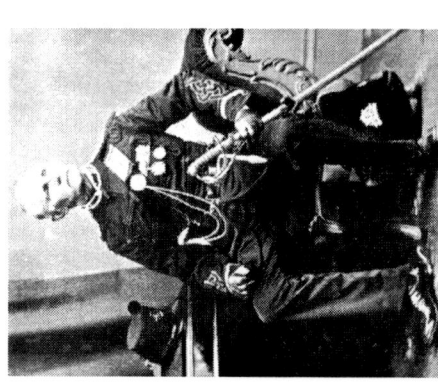

Untitled
(Suggested title "Rhenoster")

Now friends with your attention,
A story I'll relate,
About the gallant Derbys,
Who so bravely met their fate,
In the Anglo-Boer War,
When that glorious stand they made,
At the battle of Rhenoster,
When they fought De Wet's Brigade.

The Boers they did surround us,
In the middle of the night,
And then we started fighting,
Before it was daylight.
With shells they did bombard us,
And brave men's blood was shed,
For seven long hours we fought, until,
Our Colonel got shot dead.

Although we were defeated,
Still that was no disgrace.
We fought the odds of four to one,
With six big guns to face,
You'll own our men fought bravely,
And dearly sold their lives,
When they fought for Queen and Country,
Their children and their wives.

It is a well known story,
And one we shan't forget,
So tell your children's children,
Of how we fought De Wet,
With gallant Colonel Douglas,
A man who knew no fear,
When he crossed Rhenoster River,
With the Sherwood Foresters.

Unsigned.
Written about 4ᵗʰ Militia Battalion, Derbyshire Regiment. circa 1900
Found in papers of Capt Frank Brindley M.C. (who served in South Africa with the 4ᵗʰ Bn as a Sergeant and later was commissioned and served in the Great War 1914-18 with the 2/6ᵗʰ Battalion)

DEATH OF SERGEANT PERKINS

Draw down the blinds, and toll the minute bell,
For one 'as passed away, we all respected well;
His courage took him from us unto a foreign shore,
He fought the fight, his duty's done, to us he is no more.

'Twas hard to die so far away, no wife was by his side.
But England's sons they know no fear, whatever may betide,
No greater love no man can have than lay his own life down
In honour of our gracious Queen, his country, and her crown.

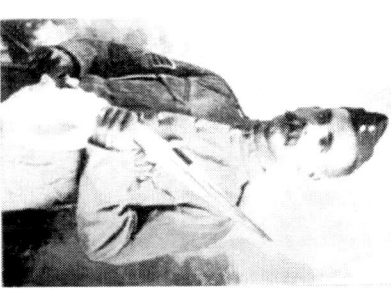

7409 Sergeant William Henry Perkins 2ⁿᵈ Volunteer Battalion. Killed in action at Rhenoster River Cape Colony, South Africa when serving with the 4ᵗʰ Battalion 7ᵗʰ June 1900. Buried at Rhenoster, South Africa.

With those that weep we sympathise, but now his soul's at rest,
To wife and friends, we know 'tis hard, but perhaps 'tis for the best,
He's done his duty well, we know, though pain to us be given,
There's yet one ray of hope for her, to meet him safe in Heaven.
'Twas hard to struggle there alone, no friend to say good bye,
No wife nor mother by his side to close his dying eye.
We know his duty he had done, though hard it was to fall,
His spirit's now across the bar, he's answered death's roll call.

Then let us one and all unite a monument to provide,
That all may read as they pass by, how our brave hero died,
And when his comrades shall return with the sad news to tell,
How bravely their dear comrade fought, and like a soldier fell.

Signed G.H. Perkins (Subject's brother),

Relating to 7409 Sergeant William Henry Perkins 2nd Volunteer Battalion

From newscutting printed in Buxton advertiser, dated Oct. 27th 1900, and in the file of Sgt Perkins

Then came the Great War of 1914-18

HAVE YOU FORGOTTEN YVONNE

Where the Flemish poplars line the cobbled street,
Yvonne hears the march of phantom feet,
And the soldier's songs of far off yesterday,
Seem to pass by the old café,
That same dream each night comes to her,
Maybe you don't remember.

Have you forgotten Yvonne, and her estaminet
On the hill,
All through her dreams, she can hear you,
Singing Tipperary still.
By the long road that leads up to Arras,
She waits like she used to do,
Though you may have forgotten Yvonne,
She has never forgotten you.

Green the grass is growing, where the earth was grey,
Green the brass cap badge, she'd hid away,
Hears the drums throbbing through the rain,
All her dreams are the same somehow,
Is she forgotten now?

**Unsigned, in papers of Lieutenant Colonel,
V.O.Robinson M.C. and two bars
(circa 1st World War.)**

"GETTING COMFY"
(A "Poem" from the 3/5th)

Here we are a few of the boys,
All merry and gay with joy.
We arrived at Grantham at mid-day,
All of us singing the ditty "Hooray".

When we started off for Camp,
Full three miles we had to tramp.
But when we saw our huts we shouted with delight,
Some of the boys they did say a pint they could drink outright!

There's 26 in one hut, so bet we have so fun,
Another thing I've got to say is we've found a place for each gun,
All that we want now is a few old washerwomen,
Who for us our clothes will wash quite willing.

When our fill we do not get,
We're off to the canteen you can bet,
There nice things we get alright,
And for them we do not have to fight.

Anything for our Major we will do,
Now he's the man to see us through,
Of our Captains we think a lot,
Because he knows what good men he has got.

**Mustard,
C.Company**

The next six poems were all written by 18032 Corporal E. F. G. Stevenson.10th Battn. circa 1915.

Cpl Ewart Ferney Gervaise Stevenson (above)
Enlisted in 10th Battalion "C" Coy in 1914 - he became Corporal 18032 - went to France with the Battalion on 15/7/1915
Wounded at Ypres late 1915 - Was in hospital in England in 1916
Awarded a conspicuous gallantry card for actions on the 10th-12th Oct 1917
Commissioned in 10th Bn 26/2/1919
Holds 1914-15 Star, British War Medal, Victory Medal, 39-45 Defence Medal. (Home Guard)

YPRES TRENCHES. December 1915.

Some speak the joys of nicotine
While lolling by the fire,
There contemplating life serene
Observe the smoke aspire,
But we who man the muddy trench
This bitter winter weather,
When cold winds howl and rain storms drench
Both friend and foe together,
We feel the need of some solace
To charm a dismal scene,
To lift us from this awful place
And give the mind serene.

Then pipe bowls glow, blue smoke hangs low,
Fond home gleams through the haze.
All, held dear creep very near,
We feel the firelight blaze,
Then memory's knack of harking back
Recalls past peaceful scenes.
Forgotten quite our sorry plight
Enraptured in our dreams.
Here! Have a pipe of mine.

BOMBING.

We buy a penny candle and light it in the tent.
Old Fritz comes sailing overhead on villainy intent.
The cry goes up "Put out the lights",
And meekly we comply,
And curse old Fritz and all his tricks
And wait his passing by.

We hear the buzzing overhead,
We hear him lay the eggs.
"He's clear away" someone will say.
Illumination begs,
We light the candles once again,
And matches are so scarce.

When "Put those lights out" someone yells,
We do and madly curse.
If all the planes that Fritz has got,
And all his bombs as well,
Would find the place we wish them in,
You'd find 'em all in Hell.

TIS A WEARY WICKED WORLD

'Tis a weary wicked world,
and it's full of wicked ways.
In the midst of it we're hurl'd,
For a numbered length of days.
We pine and weep and curse the fate,
That made us so disconsolate.
And miserably sit and sigh,
Anticipating trouble nigh.
Then when it comes cry,
Heaven preserve us from the stroke we so deserve.
Oft trouble comes and oft before,
We feel it's might t'is passed and o'er.
So throw all gloomy thoughts behind,
Still life is sweet, till friends are kind.
To life and friendship give your best,
And leave to Providence the rest.

BERTHA

When Bertha asked her brother Bob,
To write in her autograph book,
The section wishing to be in the job,
Most eagerly undertook.

To furnish the copy, one page each man,
Trusting that Bertha whenever she scan,
The scrawl that we write,
The verse we indite,
The views that we sketch with such a delight,
Will remember Observers by day or by night.

Sitting in shell holes eye deep in mud,
Sleeping in dug outs on beds of soft wood,
Doing their bit on indifferent grub,
At the explicit orders of some junior sub,
And cursing the while with unholy delight.

We're a long time away,
But the job's to be done,
Though some people say,
Duration will come.

It may do tomorrow,
May be months,
May be years,
Cheer O banish sorrow,
There's someone who cares.

TO MR PEADON

There's a peaceful old world township far away.
There's a happy home stands adown the street.
All those happy smiling faces in my mind appear today.
As I conjure times gone by to memory sweet,
There was wit and jocund laughter,
There was happiness and fun,
There was lovers delight and all the joy of youth.
Ah the hours that sped too quickly ere our mirth had well begun.
Ah the time when peace and goodwill seemed Christ's truth.

The times are strangely altered, all the land immersed in war.
All our thoughts are centred wholly upon strife,
And we sacrifice creation to an ever gaping maw,
That drains with greed unsatisfied, our life.
All the joy of Christmas altered, all the thoughts of peace and love
Seem dead, but yet the yearning never dies.
And we hope with hearts a longing and out thoughts upturned above,
For the time when peace shall wing us from the skies.

There's a peaceful old world township far away.
There's a happy home that stands a down the street.
So when all this strife is over may our faces blithe and gay,
In fond and happy times once more meet.

OBSERVERS.

Twelve fine Observers paraded smart and clean,
The pride of all the Foresters easy to be seen.
A lusty body brave and bold, and never known to fear. They marched into the line one day,
What happened just read here,

Twelve fine Observers the army's salt n' leven.
One went into hospital,
that left eleven.

Eleven bold Observers up to the line again.
One was under brigade,
then there were ten.

Ten brave Observers, nearer to the line,
One got rather windy,
Then there were nine.

Nine smart Observers, daring any fate,
Fizz came a whizz-bang,
then there were eight.

Eight pale Observers, on fatigue were down,
One fell in a shell hole,
Then there were seven.

Seven wet Observers, in a muddy fix,
One lost connection,
Then there were six.

Six wild Observers, buzzing like a hive,
One slyly buzzed off,
Then there were five.

Five fagged Observers, cursing more and more,
One cursed an R.S.M,
Then there were four.

Four dry Observers, smelled the rum with glee,
One supped the issue,
Then there were three.

Three pale Observers, don't know what to do,
One pinched the C.O.'s rum,
Then there were two.

Two bright Observers, spotting for a gun,
Zonk came a mortar,
Then there was one.

One lone Observer, said this jobs no fun,
Rejoined his blooming Company,
And now there are none.

2nd Lieut E.F.G. Stevenson 1919

OUR SAM

You've heard about Sam and his musket,
And how, when it fell on the ground,
He defied both the Sergeant and Captain,
Till Wellington had to come round.

But you won't have heard of the story,
That I am going to tell.
It shows how he rejoined the army,
And defeated the Germans as well.

Well, after Wellington left him,
Sam said, "I'm fed up with the guards",
So he handed in a week's notice,
And called at t' weekend for his cards.

He couldn't bear t' sight of a musket,
And swore that by hook or by crook,
That if another war started,
He'd join up next time as a cook.

So when we had trouble wi' t Germans,
Sam answered the call right away,
And joined up in t' Second Sixth Sherwoods,
A grand lot of chaps in their day.

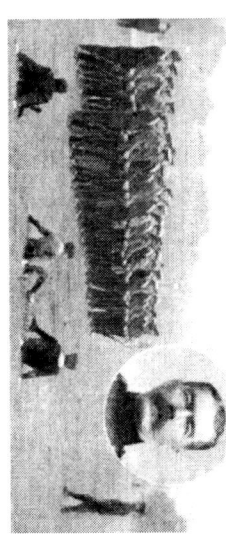

Britain's New Army of Freedom

He applied for a job in the Cookhouse,
Of cooking, he'd always done ample,
And along with his short application,
Sent one of his pies as a sample.

The Colonel just tasted one mouthful,
And said, "Oh! This Garside's no dunce,
Put him in charge of the Cookhouse,
And make him a Sergeant at once."

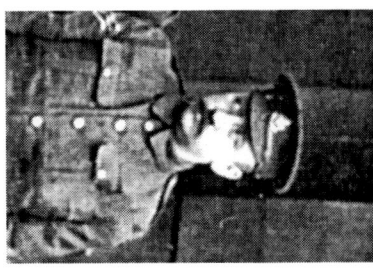

240760 Sgt Sam Garside 2/6ᵗʰ Bn

But trouble was only just started,
And really to t' Colonel's surprise,
They couldn't find any Cookhouse,
That would hold a man of Sam's size.

But Sam was a native of Buxton,
And knowing the district quite well,
Said, "Colonel, there's no need to worry,
They've got one at t' Empire Hotel."

So that's why we went up to Buxton,
It wasn't for the sake of our health,
But just because of that Cookhouse,
It's true! 'Cos Sam told me himself.

Sam's cooking had soon become famous,
And not without cause, I must own.
Since he started to cook for the Sherwoods,
Indigestion had never been known.

It was while he was on Active Service,
He came to the notice of Foch,
His fame had spread even farther,
He was known to the enemy Bosche.

Now t' Kaiser had heard about Garside,
And also his bully beef stew,
And thought if he took Sam a prisoner,
He'd cook him a basinful too.

So he called all his Army Commanders,
It was March, in Nineteen Eighteen.
They decided to launch an offensive,
The like of which was never seen.

Old Sam was made their objective,
In t' battle, some thousands were tossed,
They weren't worried about Haig and all t' others,
But Sam must be caught at all cost.

Before Sam realized what had happened,
There were dozens of Germans around,
It was t' first time he'd longed for his musket,
Since that day when it lay on the ground.

"At last we have got Sgt. Garside",
A Bosche Officer started to bawl.
"It looks a lot like it", said Sammy,
"And I see you've got Drury an' all."

So now he was taken a captive,
And to cut a long story short,
He was taken along to the Kaiser,
Where Sam told him just what he thought.

The Kaiser

But t' Kaiser was in a good humour,
Although Sam was still in a huff,
And refused to cook stew and his dough boys,
But promised to make a plum duff.

They gave him the run of the kitchen,
To prepare his plum duff for the feast,
But one thing he kept as a secret,
He made the whole thing out of yeast.

The Kaiser sat down to his dumpling,
And said it was most appetizing,
While Sam sat and waited for t' fun
That would start when t' yeast started rising.

So he went out into the garden,
For the yeast would be rising quite soon,
Then the Kaiser came out for a breather,
And shot up just like a balloon.

As soon as he knew what had happened,
He shouted out something like Hock!
And Sam who was bursting with laughter,
Replied, "Well ta-ta, my old cock."

Hindenberg called in the morning,
Looking for Bill, The Almighty,
Said Sam, "Well if t' wind hasn't changed
By now, he will be somewhere near Blighty."

Now the Kaiser was feeling quite poorly,
His face was the colour of grass,
Several times he repeated,
And so let out most of the gas.

He parted with some of his ballast,
And came down to earth in fine style,
And found he had landed in Holland,
Where he's kept to this day in exile.

When Hindenberg knew he'd lost t' Kaiser,
The end of the fight, he foresaw,
And said, "It's that cook Sergeant Garside,
That's won the for the Allies, the War."

Folk still think Old Bill abdicated,
It's quite time the real truth was known.
It was Sam and his yeast and his dumpling,
That blew Kaiser Bill from his throne.

Well, having got t' war safely over,
Sam settled down just like the rest,
And turns up each year to the Dinner,
To have a few drinks and a jest.

We on our part, are all hoping,
That he will be spared for some time,
To tell us about the adventures,
That happened to him in his prime.

H.A.Brown.
(Lieutenant, 2nd Battn (D.C.M.)

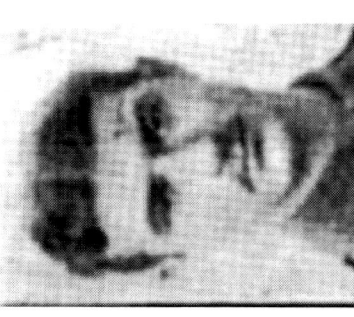

Lieut H. A. Brown, Served in the Ranks, Sergeant, Acting Company Sergeant Major, (240790) 2nd Battalion The Sherwood Foresters: 2nd Lieut 31.7.1918: Awarded D.C.M. London Gazette 18.6.1917

The following two poems are in memory of Captain Sydney F. Brookfield, 17th (Welbeck Rangers) Battalion. Killed in Action at Maillet Wood 3.9.1916, No known Grave, commemorated Thiepval Memorial, Somme, France.

Wisely he watched, and judged with fearless pen,
The players in the mimic Life of Art;
Till came the call from Life itself, and then,
Nobly on that high stage he played his part.

By: Sir Owen Seaman.
(For the portrait which is hung in the hall of the Institute of Journalists.)

TO LIEUTENANT PELLINORE

You will pardon me, I pray, Pellinore,
If I cannot come to say Au revoir,
For I had to go instead,
To an influenza bed,
With a devil of a head, Pellinore!

Do I see in this idea, Pellinore,
Of your going to the Theatre of War,
Your deliberate "intench",
To support the drama French,
And all German farce to quench, Pellinore?

Whatsoever be your game, Pellinore,
May you never, never aim, but to score!
Which, so far as I can see,
Ought not very hard to be,
With yourself as "Referee", Pellinore!

Of your courage we've no doubt, Pellinore,
For we've seen you sitting out, by the score,
Fresh attempts at Shakespeare's "Kings"
Where the "tin of battle" rings,
Like one's culinary things,
Gone to war!

And we've known you, by the way, Pellinore,
Brave a Melville khaki play!
Furthermore, you've been very near "the front",
Sitting calm (as is your wont),
With no weapon but a blunt Kohinoor!

So I drink to you, my buck, Pellinore,
In ammoniated muck I abhor!
Which must show you how sincere,
Are the hopes I'm hoping here,
For your luck in the New Year, Pellinore!

Signed L.G.T.
(Written by a dramatic critic friend of Sydney Brookfield and read at the "Au Revoir" dinner, given by the Critics' Circle to their colleague. The name 'Pellinore' relates to Brookfield's sobriquet when writing in "The Referee")

Captain Sydney Freeman Brookfield Commissioned into the Border Regiment in 1914, Transferred to 17th (Welbeck Rangers) Battalion The Sherwood Foresters November 1915.

Four poems by Edwin Hudson.
Father of 107690 Pte .J Hudson,
and 268203 Pte. W. T. Hudson,

17/3/17

If Mayfields byegone worthys,
Could pup at Mayfield now,
Observe the changes that are made,
And note the "why" and "how",
Their heads would shake in sadness,
And truthfully they'd say,
Your alterations have not been
Improvements every way.

When Tom Moore lived at Stancliffe,
And wrote those Evening Bells,
The parish had no waterworks
But drew its drink from wells,
It may have been unsightly
And gave food ground for fleas,
But folks as happy were as now,
And lived as many years.

Their winters were as long as ours,
Their summers were as wet,
Their farmers said that corn was dear,
And hay was hard to get.
But if you'd lived Oake's time,
And milk at Harlow bought,
It cost no more a gallon then,
Than now it costs a quart.

No more shall see them sent to face,
Another nation's guns.
When nations rule with acts of love,
And not by force of arms,
When Christian homes and harvest fields,
Are freed from wars alarms.
When man resolves with brother man,
To keep the precept true:
Do unto others as you would that they do to you.

Edwin.Hudson, 1916.

PEACE BELLS

When we get our daily paper,
What a joy it is to find,
That the Allies are successful,
That our efforts still combined,
In one great and grand endeavor.
To establish truth and right
Have met with no reverses,
But are gaining in the fight.

That the submarine which threatened
To cut off our food supplies,
And the Zeppelins which menaced
With destruction from the skies,
Have met superior forces,
Eer they'd met time to work their will…

…But twill be a greater pleasure,
when we hear the peace bells ring.
As from every parish steeple,
They the welcome tidings fling.
That the dawn at last has broken,
Through the night so long and black
That the remnant of our soldier lads,
Will soon be coming back.

That this man-made war is over,
That the aged are relieved,
From their nightly dread of air raids,
That the prisoners are reprieved,
Who have languished long in German Camps,
And lacked both friends and food…

…When the bells ring out through Christendom,
To celebrate the peace,
May that era dawn on Christendom
When man-made wars shall cease.
When the tender patient mothers,
Who in love have borne their sons,

107690 Pte Joseph Hudson 10th Battalion killed in action when attacking the German trenches near Poix Du Nord France 4.11.1918, Buried Cross Roads British Military Cemetery, France

THERE'S A POWER

There's a power that gives men courage,
And directs and keeps them straight,
In the path of truth and duty,
Through their early years and late.
It is stronger than the impulse,
Moved by oratory or art,
And the lowliest and the mightiest,
In its guidance have a part.
Yet it operates in silence,
From their cradle all through life,
'Tis the influence of our women,
Mother, Sister, Sweetheart, Wife.

Of our soldiers and our sailors,
We oft speak in words of praise,
And the stories of our airmen,
Will resound through all our days.
We recount their deeds of valour,
Us all think upon the past,
And their names will live in history,
Long as history shall last.
But the all pervading haven,
Which inspired their heart and mind,
Was the influence of the women,
They had loved and left behind.

Far away on land contending,
In the air or on the wave,
Out to keep our land inviolate,
'Gainst the huns who seek to strafe.
Where so'er they may be fighting,
Through the whole worlds length or breadth,
Each one feels some woman's influence,

Is to him a tower of strength.
Ever present, ever constant,
Ever prompting him for good,
What each owes to woman's influence,
He'll ne'er tell nor ever could.

Original Grave of 268203 Private William T. Hudson 2nd Battalion killed in action in the trenches at Kemmel, Belgium. Buried Nine Elms British Military Cemetery, Poperinghe, Belgium

A TRIBUTE TO OUR TERRIERS

At the dawn of a Sunday morning
In July Nineteen One Four,
A bugle sound gave warning,
Reveille was heard at the door.
'Twas a call to the lads of Mayfield,
Who had offered to take their part
If Old England should need protection,
To defend her with hand and heart.

They had taken an oath in peacetime,
That if ever the future should bring,
An enemy host to invade us,
They would fight for our Country and King.
And on Saturdays after dinner,
And evenings wet or fine,
They would clean their gun, put khaki on,
And go training for the line.

They have given their leisure for training,
They have learned to march and shoot,
They have learned to be uncomplaining,
They had learned to "endure and be mute",
And they rise at the call of the bugle,
And with rifle and pack they tramp,
To join their comrades at Ashbourne,
For the Terriers Annual Camp.

They had just settled down to Camp life,
When comes the terrible word,
"The peace of Europe is broken,
The Kaiser has drawn the sword."
And their camp is quietly broken,
And back to their homes they repair,
To await the summons for action,
And be ready to do and dare.

Next day they are on active service
And a thirty mile march they make,
From the market place at Ashbourne
To Headquarters: their place to take
With their comrades from Clay Cross and Buxton,
From Bakewell and Wirksworth and Clowne,
And a gallant array of pit lads,
From Staveley and Chesterfield Town.

And now the Sixth Sherwoods are mustered,
And their thoughts are lifted higher,
When their Colours they take, for safe keeping,
To the church with the crooked spire.
And the Canon is there to meet them,
And he gives them this message bright
"Though you fight for King and Country,
you fight first for God and Right."

And he prays that the God of battles
May guard and protect them all,
That in pity and infinite mercy,
He will comfort those who may fall.
And the Terriers attentively kneeling,
From the depth of their feeling when
At the end of his prayer they respond with,
A reverent clear "Amen."

Six months are now spent in field service,
With a life in the open air,
Maneuvering, and shooting and trenching,
On hill sides brown and bare.
In improving the country's defences
And guarding against a surprise,
As they pick up the trick of the Britisher quick,
In the bayonet exercise.

Meanwhile our contemptible army,
Had stopped the German's advance,
But their ranks had suffered severely
And more men were needed in France.

And the Terriers willing and eager,
To help crush the Prussian pride,
Volunteered to a man to be sent to the van,
To fight by the "Regular's" side.

Since then they've been fighting our battles,
And stopping the German's rush,
While for days at a time in the trenches,
They had stood in the mud and slush.
They had stood to the waist in water,
They have known the feel of trench feet
And when the shells have dropped thick in their quarter,
They had had none too much to eat.

They have faced the deadly sniper,
And the high explosive shell,
And through the long night watches,
They had guarded the parapet well.
They have fought at Loo's and Hullack
And their pluck, was rewarded when
Hohenzollern redoubts gave way to the shout
and the charge of the Terrier men.

But some have come back to the Homeland,
Broken in body and health,
And to these let us all be grateful,
Nor grudge them a share of our wealth.
They have fought for the homes and children,
Of every one in the land,
And while we can work we never should shirk
To give them a helping hand.

And some will come back to us never,
They are gone beyond our recall,
In the nations great endeavour,
They truly have given their all.
But their memory will live with us ever,
Their example our conduct enhance,

For like heroes they died in their young manhood's pride
In the struggle of Belgium and France.

And some are still fighting for Freedom,
For Liberty, Justice and Truth.
And we trust that God will watch o'er them,
As He did o'er the shepherd youth.
And though we extol the Terriers,
We remember they're only a part
Of the gallant heroic army,
So dear to the Nation's heart.

Edwin Hudson, 1915.

IN THE COULDRON

Taters in the cauldron sink
Peeled by hand as black as ink,
Portions of a slaughtered cat,
Piece of breakfast bacon fat,

Bits of boot and bits of stick
Make the gruel good and thick
German sausage won in fight
On some dark and stormy night,

Dim and murky watercress
Stolen from a Sergeants' mess,
Slabs of cheese and chunks of ham,
Lumps of plumb and apple jam,

Bits of paper, ends of string,
Mixed with any damned thing,
In the cauldron mingle quick,
So the stew be dense and thick.

Anon
Extracted from the book 'C' Coy 1/5th Battalion
Battle of 100 days.

ON THE RED RED ROAD TO HOOGE

On parade- get your spade.
Fall in, the pick and shovel brigade.
There's a carrying fatigue for half a league,
And work to do with the spade.
Through the dust and ruins of Ypres town,
The seventeen inch still battering down,
Sweeping death with it's fiery breath,
On the red, red, road to Hooge.

Who is the one who's time has come,
Who won't return when the work is done,
Who will leave his bones on the blood stained stones,
On the red, red road to Hooge?
Onward the Foresters and never a stop,
To the sandbagged trench and over the top,
Over the top if a bullet you stop,
On the red, red, road to Hooge.

The burst and roar of the hand grenade,
Welcome us on to the death parade,
The pit of gloom- the valley of doom,
The crater down at Hooge.
Full many a soldier from the Rhine,
Must sleep tonight in a bed of lime,
'Tis a pitiless grave for brave or knave,
In the crater down at Hooge.

Hark to the "Stand to" fusillade,
Sling your rifle, bring your spade,
And fade away, ere the break of day,
Or a hole you'll fill at Hooge.
Call the roll, and another name,
Is sent to swell the roll of fame.
So we carve a cross to mark the loss,
Of a chum who fell at Hooge.

Not a deed for the paper man to write,
No glorious charge in the cawning light,
The Daily Mail won't tell the tale,
Of the night work down at Hooge.
But our General knows and his praise we've won,
He's pleased with the work the Foresters have done,
In the shot and shell at the Gates of Hell,
On the red, red, road to Hooge.

Found in papers of
2nd Lieutenant, Thomas Moore Emmanuel Ward.
12th Pioneer Battalion 1916

Three poems by Corporal Brand
7th Robin Hood Battalion
Circa 1915-16

BRAVO ROBIN HOODS

"Bravo! Robin Hoods."
This message so fine, once flashed o'er the line,
From a city far over the sea,
To its men at the front, who were bearing the brunt,
Of the battles that meant liberty.
They had heard, so they say, in a casual way,
Of a fight that took place there one night,
Of a mad German raid, trenches lost it was said,
And supports rushing up to the fight.

There were cheers from the Huns, and the roaring of guns,
And shells that burst high in the air;
Our front line was scattered, our trenches were battered,
And help's badly needed up there.
Then the men in support came along as they ought,
And they say the achievement was fine,
And though lots of men fell, and the Colonel as well,
They succeeded in holding the line.

SOLDIER'S OF YPRES 1914-1915

"Who comes?
Who gives our password with the right to join our ranks?"
"Soldiers of England."
"Nay, not these, we know our own.
No host like this bore arms for England."
"Yet we are her sons."
"Whence come you?"
"From your Calvary of Ypres."
"That holy spot where valour reached a height,
And unsupported, held and saved the world.
You came more nearly to the high ideal
Of one who died for men, than e'er you dreamed,
There, where for God and Right- naught else- you raised
The Standard in the face of awful odds,
One watchword only, 'Duty' on your lips"
"Now God be thanked, and be you welcome- friends!"

Unsigned.
Extracted from Battalion History of 1/7 Battn

TO THE PRESENT OCCUPIERS

Hearken all ye whom duty calls,
To spend some time within these friendly walls,
Others will sojourn here when you have passed,
You were not first and you will not be last,
Therefore take heed and do whate'er you may,
For safety and for comfort while you stay,

Just put a sandbag here, a picture there,
To make a room more safe, a wall less bare:
Think as you tread the thorny path of duty,
Of comfort, of security and beauty,
So your successors when they come may say,
"A splendid unit we relieved today."

Found in papers of,
2nd Lieutenant Thomas Moore Emmanuel Ward.
12th Pioneer Battalion, 1916

TO THE HOHENZOLLERN REDOUBT
(Stormed by the North Midland Division, October 13th 1915)

Oh proud Hohenzollern, named after a King,
You stood in your sullen might,
And a challenge to all British arms did fling,
Caring little for pity and right,
Machine gunned and wired, your strength was well known.
You were manned by a terrible crew,
But little you knew, oh mighty Redoubt,
What the "Terrier" men could do.

And you won't forget that October day,
That sounded your funeral knell,
'Twas heard in the roar of the British guns,
and the scream of the British shells.
They broke your defences and splintered the wire,
With a fury no power could stop,
And you read your doom in that line of steel,
When the "Boys" went over "the top."

And long you'll remember that Staffordshire rash,
And the Lincoln and Leicestershire attack,
Though you tore up their ranks with a deadly fire,
You failed to drive them back;
Though the ground was covered with British dead.
They advanced through your trenches, and then
Your last chance vanished when "over the top"
Came the Notts. and Derby men.

Oh men from the Midlands, the people at home
Are proud of your courage and skill,
And in long years to come, the tale of your deeds
Will re-echo o'er Derbyshire hills.
In the Pottery towns and the valleys of Trent,
And over the Lincolnshire Fen,
They will tell of the big Redoubt
That was stormed by the "Terrier" men.

Corporal Brand 7th Robin Hood Battalion 1915

Then to check German advances, and spoil all their chances,
A trench must be dug in their face;
And in spite of their ire, 'twas dug under fire,
Whilst our guns held them up in their place.
And it made the foe frown to see men digging down,
In spite of their efforts to "strafe";
And when bullets flew from this trench then they knew,
That the British position was safe.

Oh! Afternoons spent in your firing at Trent,
And evenings all took up by drill,
And the long weary tramp on your way back to camp,
As you marched over valley and hill:
It may have seemed vain as you "sloshed" through the rain,
But we know now our men are the "goods",
And by holding the line, get this message so fine,
"Bravo! Robin Hoods."

Corporal Brand 7th Battalion, circa 1916

IN MEMORY OF SGT REGINALD GRUNDY

There is a dove what flies above
And never loses a feather.

If I cannot have the one I love
I will go without forever.

By Edith Dorothy Wallis.
In memory of Reginald Grundy.
Sergeant, 7th Battalion. 1st World War.
A verse from the diary of Reginald Grundy's Fiancée, Edith Wallis, dated October 1915 on his death. She remained a spinster till dying aged 75.

715 Sergeant Reginald Horace Grundy
Killed in Action 1.10.1915 when the Germans exploded a mine under the trench near Verbanden Molen, Belgium. Buried Hedge Row Cemetery, Belgium

THE CITIZEN SOLDIER

There's a pal of Tommy Atkins I would introduce to you,
He's not a first-class soldier I'll confess;
He's called a Territorial, and when there's work to do,
You'll find he's hard to conquer or depress.
You've never thought much of these men before,
But I want you to look at them now-
Pulling their guns through the rain and the mud,
Or driving them over a ridge.
Or an Infantry picquet, wet through to the skin,
Or Yeomanry guarding a bridge.
In spite of the sneers they stick to the work,
They belong to a stubborn race;
And when England's in danger and sounds the "fall-in",
Then we find every man in his place.

He gets home in the evening feeling tired of it all,
For it's hard work in a coal mine, or a mill;
And whilst you are getting ready for a whist drive or a ball,
He spends his evening learning how to drill,
But I want you to look at the now-
Feeding their horses at break of day,
When the cold is turning them blue;
Or guarding a lonely magazine,
Or pulling their rifles through.
They are only "tin-pot" soldiers,
No good for a Show Parade;
But they buckle their marching order on,
When old England needs their aid.

He has volunteered for service, for he hears the battle cry,
And you'll find that he is one, who never runs,
When he hears the deadly whistle of the bullets going by,
You've never thought much of these men before,
But I want you to look at them now-
Digging a trench on the Eastern coast,
Ankle deep in the mud;
Or the charge of the London Scottish,
Their bayonets red with blood.
Or marching along 'neath an Indian sky,
Or through English mist and rain;
So just line the streets and give them a cheer,
When the boys march home again.

Corporal Brand 7th Battalion, circa 1916

UNTITLED

Heedless and careless, still the world goes on,
And leaves us broken- Oh! Our sons!
Our sons!
Yet think of this!
Yea, rather think of this!
He died as few men get the chance to die,
Fighting to save a world's morality.
He died the noblest death a man may die,
Fighting for god, and Right, and Liberty.
And such a death is Immortality

Anon.
In memory of Lieutenant E.H.N. Cordeux, 7th Battalion, 1st World War.

Extract from Battalion History of 1/7 Battn. (The Robin Hoods) The Sherwood Foresters, found in papers of Sergeant R. Grundy, 7th Battn.

SHERWOODS IN BELLINGLIESE

They were only Territorials,
But soldiers tried and true,
Who had "done their bit" in trenches,
To storming, they were new.

Still to dangers, trials and hardships,
They were old hands at the game,
And no line Regiment need be shamed, if their record is the same.

But now the flower of prowess, they'll put in their archives,
How they stormed one misty morning,
And captured Bellenglise.
'Twas impossible, it had been said, to storm and take the place,
With it's natural strength of hills all round, no troops could ever face.

To add to this, machine guns had reign of vantage great,
From every knoll and hillside, with scarcely any break,
Command the whole position, and could sweep with greatest ease,
All those who tried to capture "Historic Bellenglise."

They rushed across a rotten bridge, 'twas hanging by a thread,
In time to catch the engineers, and quickly shot them dead.
One minute more, and sure enough, they'd have blown the bridge to hell,
And perhaps have wiped the Sherwood's out before the village fell.

Their appetite for fighting, now, there's nothing could appease,
Except the fall and capture of "famous Bellenglise."

Signed, 'C.Cartwright, Regimental Tailor, 8th Sherwood Foresters, B.E.F. France', circa 1918.
In papers of V.O.Robinson (Lieut. Colonel, 6th Battalion.)

A WAIL

Life has many disappointments,
Days are never free from care,
For in spite of using ointments
Steadily I'm losing my hair.

THE GREEN HILLS OF ASHBOURNE

O dear to our hearts are the green hills of Asbourne,
The breezes blow fresh over scenes that we love,
The flower-spangles meadows, the bird haunted wild woods,
The rivulets wending their way to the Dove.

But over these fair scenes, the storm clouds were gathering,
Filling the air with war's dreadful alarms,
The signal rang out over hillside and valley,
"Your country doth need you, ye patriots, to arms."

Marching away o'er the green hills of Ashbourne,
Our brave lads were eager to answer the call,
With courage undaunted, they rushed to the conflict,
For King and for Country, to fight or to fall.

In a land far away from the green hills of Ashbourne,
Our comrades were valiantly paying the debt,
For King and for Country they fought and they conquered,
O loyal and true hearts, we shall not forget.

They are gone for a while from the green hills of Ashbourne,
Their voices no more wake the echoes around,
The Last Post has spoken, the darkness has fallen,
Our soldiers will rest till Reveille shall sound

Honour and love to the heroes who perished,
Honour and love to the patriot band,
On the green hills of Ashbourne their names will be cherished,
While those hills in their grandeur and beauty shall stand.

By Miss L. Sinfield, Sunday School teacher and member of St.John's C.E. Church, Asbourne.

**The Sinfield sisters
Miss L. Sinfield the composer of this poem is seated on the left**

THE WIPERS TIMES

The wipers times was published by a group of officers NCO's and men of the 12th (Pioneer) Battalion The Sherwood Foresters, under the editorship of Capt F.J. Roberts M.C. It made its first appearance in February 1916 when the battalion were living in the Ramparts of Ypres. It moved with the battalion and changed its name to The Somme Times, The New Church Times, The Kemmel Times changing to The B.E.F. Times and finally The Better Times.

As the paper was published by the 12th Battalion The Sherwood Foresters and because we have many of the original papers in the archive, here include are a number of poems covering the period 1914-18, which were written by men of the battalion or by officers and men associated with it and "living" nearby. Credits are given in the format originallyprinted as and when they appear in the Wipers Times.

VIEWS OF THE "EDITORIAL SANCTUM" AS IT WAS IN 1916 AND IS TODAY

The casements set within the Wipers ramparts, the centre one was where the Wipers Times was eventually printed and was the 'Home' of Capt Roberts.

Captain F. J. Roberts M.C.
12th (Pioneer) Battalion
Editor of "The Wipers Times"

The same casement to-day

It is not the task here to highlight the effect the paper had on the troops, but needless to say it was always very well sought after and was the source of great amusement to many, including the General Staff. The paper contained hundreds of assorted snippets, humorous advertisements and also many poems.

THE RATION CARRIERS

On the road from Pop. To Bosinghe
And from Bosinghe down to Ypres
Where the pave's rent with Johnson
And the mud just ankle deep
Where you darsn't light a fag up
'Cos the Boche's eyes are skinned
Ah, thats the place to be boys,
If you want to raise a wind.

When the roads all blocked with transport
Taking rations to the dump,
And they're shelling Dawsons Corner
With shrapnel and with crump,
When the word comes down the column
"A stretcher bearer quick!"
Then your mouth goes kind of dry boys,
And your stomach's awful sick.

When you hear a sort of whistle
That swells into a roar,
And yer ducks, yer ducks like Hell, Boys!
'Cos you've heard that sound before.
There's a crash that echoes skywards,
And a scream of mortal pain
Then you curse the blasted Kaiser
And just march on again.

So you chaps back in Blighty
Who have'nt got the grit
To go and take the shilling,
And to come and do your bit,
Just now and then remember
At night time, 'ere you sleep
The men who carry rations
On the road from Pop. to Ypres.
D.H.R.

STOP GAP

Little stacks of sandbags,
Little lumps of clay;
Make our blooming trenches,
In which we work and play.

Merry little wiz-bang,
Jolly little crump;
Made our trench a picture,
Wiggle, Woggle, Wump.

*****

The corp'rl and the privit they
Was standing in the road.
Do you suppose, the corp'rl said,
That rum is "A la mode?"
I doubt it ! said the privit as
He shouldered up his load.

"Now this ere war, the corp'rl said,
Has lasted long enuff"
"Gorblime" said the privit with
His voice exceeding gruff,
"Not arf it aint!" and drew his nose
Across hs sheepskin cuff.

*****

An awful thought has come to me
Odd sad disaster that might be;
Just suppose a 12 inch shell
Fell right on this dug-out – well;
This train of thought I'll not pursue

(That fills the gap, and so will do)

WAR

Take a wilderness of ruin,
Spread with mud quite six feet deep;
In this mud now cut some channels,
Then you have the line we keep.

Now you get some wire that's spiky,
Throw it round outside you line;
Get some pickets, drive in tightly,
And round these your wire entwine.

Get a lot of Huns and plant them,
In a ditch across the way;
Now you have war in the making,
As waged here from day to day.

Early morn the same old "stand to"
Daylight, sniping in full swing;
Forenoon, just the merry whiz-bang,
Mid-day oft a truce doth bring.

Afternoon repeats the morning,
Evening falls then work begins;
Each works in his muddy furrow,
Set with boards to catch your shins.

Choc a block with working parties,
Or with rations coming up;
Four hours scramble, then to dug-out,
Mud encased, yet keen to sup.

Oft we're told "Remember Belgium,"
In the years that are to be;
Crosses set by all her ditches,
Are our pledge to memory.

LOVE AND WAR

In the line a soldiers fancy
Oft may turn to thoughts of love.
But too hard to dream of Nancy
When the whiz-bangs sing above.

In the midst of some sweet picture
Vision of a love swept mind,
Bang! ' A whiz-bang almost nicked yer!'
"Duck yer blighter, are yer blind?"

Take the case of poor Bill 'Arris
Deep in love with Rosy Greet,
So forgot to grease his tootsies,
Stayed outside and got "Trench Feet."

Then remember old Tom Stoner,
Ponder on his awful fate.
Always writing to his Donah,
Lost is rum 'cos E was late.

Then again there's 'Arry 'Awkins,
Stopped to dream at Gordon Farm
Got a "Blightie" found his Polly
Walking out on Johnson's arm.

Plenty more of such examples
I could give, had I but time.
War on tender feelings tramples,
H.E. breaks up thoughts sublime.

"Don't dream when you're near machine guns!"
Is a thing to bear in mind.
Think of love when not between Huns,
A sniper's quick and love is blind.

SOME KNOWLEDGE

Way back from home
Across the foam
For Hunnish blood a-thirsting,
Came Captain Bass
(As green as grass)
With knowledge simply bursting

In training days
His studious ways
Caused all to gaze in wonder,
On field days long
When all went wrong
He never seemed to blunder.

Now strange to say
The very day
That Bass arrived in Flanders,
Another too
Arrived at "Q"
His name was Percy Sanders.

How different he
Appeared to be
In contrast to our hero,
He did not roar
For Hunnish gore
His spirits seemed at zero.

With buttons bright
And Sam Browne tight
This twain went into battle,
How happy they
Upon that day
How sweet their childish prattle.

My simple lay
I grieve to say
To ghoulish taste now panders,
For you will see
That Captain "B"
Is killed and so is Sanders.

Upon the ground
A dud they'd found
(It caused them stupifaction)
In para 3
Said Captain "B"
We'll find our course of action.

It says, I see
Said Captain "B"
In fact it gives quite clearly,
With primers dry
You blow it high
Said Captain Sanders "really!!"

It seems to me
That para 3
Is merely futile raving,
The troubles less
Continued "S"
To drop it on the paving.

And Captain "B"
Agreed with "P"
His method seemed so clear,
They'll never more
See Englands shore
They've left this mortal sphere.

SOME DREAM

In Wipers, where the whiz-bangs dance,
I mused upon the great advance.
I read (though most by heart I knew)
Ream upon ream from G and Q.
Which fearsome reading nearly done
I slept – and dreamed we smashed the Hun.
Dreamed we had left our sodden trenches –
The well-known holes, the well-known stenches-
And forward stormed for wealth and wenches.
(Even in dreams, my eagle mind
Perpended Prussia's women kind-
Deciding, if it came to shooting,
I'd rather I were shot for looting)
Rifle nor mortar, gun nor lance
Had wrought-at last-our Great Advance:
Our freshest troops, our A.S.C.
It was that gave us victory!
Yea! 'Twas the Army Safety Corps
Drowned Belgium's swamps in German gore
Wagon on wagon, team on team,
I watched their quarter-locks agleam,
Mad squadrons of my whiskied dream.
'Whips over' on each 'heavy draught'
They leaped the wire; and, leaping, laughed;
Then furious with uplifted crops
Hacked their red path through Clonmel Copse;
The while their deadly Fifty-Fives'
Took countless toll of limbs and lives,
Black columns down the Menin Road,
In endless streams their motors flowed……
Vainly, the flower of William's flock
Strove to withstand this awful shock.
No human force could hope to dam
Those waves of Plum and Apple Jam;
Bavaria's stoutest infantry
Paled at thy sugar, black with tea;
Proud Prussia, trained to meatless days,
Reeled and fled back in sheer amaze
As, joint to joint and knee to knee,
Charged home Fred Karno's Cavalry….
And now, alone, in Glencorse Wood,
Undaunted, little Willie stood,
And eyed the foe, and eyed the food:
Too long he tarried! F-sch-r smote.
Full on that gorged and greedy throat
With a faked requisition note…….
'TWAS MINE! Chill terror at my breast,
My traitor soul, in dreams, confessed;
And woke to find – not Army Scandals
But shortage in our ration candles.

GILBERT FRANKAU 13/3/1916

Little Jack Horner at hell Fire Corner
Sat down a biscuit to chew,
He didn't care for the shells that flew there,
He knew what the biscuit could do.
There came a twelve incher, but Jack didn't flinch, sir,
He grasped at his biscuit, and waited,
And then true and well, with biscuit met shell,
And the crump with a sigh detonated.

Anon

TO MY CHUM

No more we'll share the same old barn,
The same old dug-out, same old yarn,
No more a tin of bully share,
Nor split our rum by a star-shell's flare,
So long old lad.

What times we've had, both good and bad,
We've shared what shelter could be had,
The same crump-hole when the whiz-bangs shrieked,
The same old billet that always leaked,
An now – you've "stopped one."

We'd weathered the storm two winters long,
We'd managed to grin when all went wrong,
Because together we fought and fed,
Our hearts were light; but now – you're dead
And I am Mateless

UNTITLED

In dug-out cool I sit and sneeze,
Safe from a whiz-bangs mauling;
Dreams come my appetite to tease,
Fond visions which my fancy please
Of maids divine, enthralling,
And glorious times when our job's done,
My thoughts you'll echo – "Damn the Hun!"

GOOD-BYE

This poem was written on the occasion of the battalion leaving Ypres for a rest and a move to The Somme.

Farewell *Yperen! Yperen farewell
Long have I known thee, and known thee well!
Thy stoney streets, thy shell pitted square,
Looted thy houses for dug-out ware,
Looking for cellar cool and deep,
With a shell proof roof where I could sleep.

No longer need thy ways to prowl,
With ears attuned for crump's shrill howl,
'Twixt doubtful joys to hesitate,
The Menin Road, or old Lille Gate?

But in my sleep I'll dream of thee,
And always in my thoughts thou'lt be,
Perchance my fate may be to see
Another place resembling thee,
But that foretells a future warm,
Where other little devils swarm,
Thy prototype can but be – well
Why should we mince the matter – HELL.

* Yperen – The Belgian name for Wipers used here to baffle the enemy.

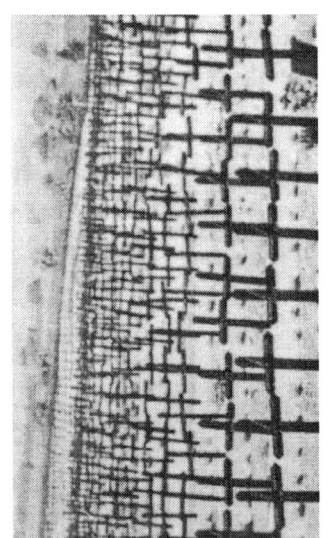

Well, old lad, here's peace to you,
And for me, well, there's my job to do,
For you and the others who lie at rest,
Assured may be that we'll do our best
In vengeance

Just one more cross by a strafed road-side,
With its G.R.G., and a name for guide,
But it's only myself who has lost a friend,
And though I may fight through to the end,
No dug-out will be the same,
All pals can only be pals in name,
But we'll all carry on till the end of the game
Because you lie there.

WHAT A HOPE

The Editor has ordered me
To write a batch of rhymes
To finish of this number of
His bally "New Church Times."

The Editor's a mighty man
His will it must be done,
I'd like to know if he can make
The clock strike less than one

Some Poet.

***

Maconochie ! Maconochie !
Bully beef and biscuits!
Hullo, damn it ! that's a crump,
How those bangs give me the hump;
Here's another ! Where's she dropping?
Duck ! or pieces you'll be stopping !
Plum and apple ! beef and biscuit,
Well, here goes, I'd better risk it;
Just round here, there is no telling
When the Hun begins his shelling
How good my dug-out seems to me.
Maconochie ! Maconochie !

SIGN POSTS

There's a line that runs from Nieuport down into Alsace Lorraine,
Its twists and turns are many, and each means a loss or gain;
Every yard can tell a story, every foot can claim its fee,
There the line will stay for ever from Lorraine up to the sea.

Though this line will be behind us as we push on to the spree,
Yet to all it will be sacred, mud encased though it may be;
In the future dim and distant they will tell the tale again –
The ghosts of those who held the line from Nieuport to Lorraine

***

Hauptmann Van Horner
In trench traverse corner,
Once heard what he thought was a "goer";
But he was mistaken
Said Fritz Carl Von Haken,
"I'll write to his widow, I know her".

SEMI-DETACHED

At a lofty elevation
Floating lazy in the sun,
What an ideal occupation
Keeping watch on brother Hun!

Though a "sausage" is my villa
Far from angry whiz-bangs' scream,
I can watch the caterpıller,
And all things are what they seem.

In a contemplative manner
When the "big push" is begun,
'Tis from here I'd love to see it
From my place up in the sun

Places memorised by symbol, little things that caught the mind,
As at Loos 'twas but a lone tree which in mem'ry is enshrined;
Perhaps at W:pers 'twas a corner, shell bespattered, held our sight,
Or a nightingale at Plug Street, sending music through the night.

Little things, yet each implanted when the nerves are tension high,
And in years to come remembered how, while gazing, death passed by;
So the line for all has sign posts, and a dug-out oft can hold
Little memories to haunt one as the future years unfold.

SPACE FILLERS

Jack and Jill on top of a Hill
Had built an O Pip Station,
But Frightful Fritz blew it to bits
To their great consternation

There was a young girl of the Somme,
Who sat on a number five bomb,
She thought 'twas a dud 'un,
But it went off sudden ---
Her exit she made with aplomb

HOW TIRPITZ WON THE BATTLE OF JUTLAND

Von Tirpitz was an admiral, his beard flew bold and free,
He called up all his captains and "My gallant lads," quoth he
"The day has come, ten thousand 'Hochs' and though I stay at home
My spirt will be with you. Now prepare to brave the foam!"

The captains tried with one accord to raise a pleasant grin,
Yet each one wondered when and how the trouble would begin;
Their ships they put in dry dock, had barnacles removed,
While by the aid of countless "steins" the outlook they improved.

"What ho, my merry mariners!" said Tirp. One day in May,
"Art ready now to sweep the sea and end Britannia's day?
Has each of you his Iron Cross, and flannel next his skin?"
With one accord they answered "Ja!"
"Gut! Now we can begin!"

So Tirpitz crept unto the gate, and peered out o'er the sea,
While gravely muttering n his beard "I'd rather you than me!"
"The coast is clear," he shouted back, "make haste 'The Day' is here!"
Then shut the gate behind them, and consoled himself with beer.

When on his homeward way he paused, this master of the gales,
And drove into his statue half a ton of six inch nails;
"Hoch! Hoch!" quoth he "now I must go and write up my report
Of this, our greatest victory, and lessons it has taught.

So he and Wolff sat down to think, and soon one came to see
The mighty German fleet had won a glorious victory,
So "wire the news around at once, the time is getting short,
The world must have our story ere our ships get back to port."

Then back went Tirp. To Kiel again and peeping through the gate
He saw some ships returning in a mighty flurried state,
"What's this?" he cried, behind his beard his face was turning pale,
And straightway to his statue went and drove another nail.
"Ho! Ho! my gallant lads," quoth he, "why make such frantic haste?
You come as though by devils chased, and little time tom waste."
The pale and shaky captains muttered through their chattering teeth
"We've won a great big vict'ry, all the foe is underneath."

"If that is so" quoth Tirpitz, "why this frantic need for haste,
Why not remain and glut on joys of which you've had a taste,
Why leave the field of victory whose laurels wreath your hair?"
"Well to be honest 'twas because the British fleet was there."

"Oh well!" sad Tirp., "the glorious news is speeding on its way,
And 'twill be known the whole world 'oer ere breaks another day;
If we can't win by ships and guns we can at least by tales."
And then into his statue drove another ton of nails.

TO THE P.B.I. (Poor Bl—— Infantry)
An appreciation

Gone is the summer and gone are the flies,
Gone the green hedges that gladdened our eyes;
Around us the landscape is reeking with rain,
Gone is all comfort – 'tis Winter again

So here's to the lads of the P.B.I.
Who live in a ditch that never is dry;
Who grin through discomfort and danger alike,
Go "over the top" when a chance comes to strike;
Though they're living in Hell they are cheery and gay,
And draw as their stipend just one bob per day.

They take what may come with a grouse just skin-deep,
In a rat worried dug-out on mud try to sleep;
Do you wonder they make all the atmosphere hum,
When some arm-chair old lunatic grudges them rum;
And they read in the papers that "James So-and-Such
Thinks that our soldiers are drinking too much."

Leave Tommy alone Mr James So-and-Such,
There are voices much nearer home waiting your touch;
Take yourself now for instance, examine and see
If your own priggish virtue is all it should be;
Give those of a larger life chance to enjoy
A charity wider than that you employ.

Don't let Tommy's vices shatter your sleep,
When you write to the "Times" stick to "Little Bo Peep,"
As a subject she's really much more in your line
Than Licentious soldiery, women and wine,
So here's to the lads who can live and can die,
Backbone of the Empire, the old P.B.I.

Pioneer

Back once more to the boots, gum, thigh,
In a pulverised trench where the mud's knee-high;
To the duck-board slide on a cold wet night,
When you pray for a star-shell to give you light;
When your clothes are wet, and the rum jar's dry,
Then you want all your cheerfulness, P.B.I.

THE WAR LORD AND THE CHANCELLOR
(With apologies to the late Lewis Carrol)

The War Lord and the Chancellor,
Were walking hand in hand;
They laughed like anything to see
The devastated land;
"If this belonged to us," they said,
"it really would be grand."

"If fifty Huns with fifty guns,
Swept it for half a year;
Do you suppose," the War Lord said,
"That victory would be near?"
"I doubt it," said the Chancellor,
And shed a bitter tear.

"You always were a pessimist,"
The frowning War Lord said;
"Oh Highest One it is because I always look ahead;
Before this war is finished you
And I will both be dead."

"Don't talk like that I do beseech,"
The War Lord wailed aloud;
"To win this War by any means,
You know that I have vowed;
With Zeppelins and submarines,
And waves of poison cloud."

"Oh chuck it Bill" the Chancellor
Said with a rueful air,
"You know quite well with 'frightfulness'
We've tried them everywhere,
And got it back with interest."
Bill glared and tore his hair.

RATS

I want to write a poem, yet I find I have no theme,
"Rats" are no subject for an elegy,
Yet they fill my waking moments, and when star-shells softly gleam,
'Tis the rats who spend the midnight hours with me.

On my table in the evening they will form "Battalion mass,"
They will open tins of bully with their teeth,
And should a cake be sent me by some friend at home, alas!
They will extricate it from its cardboard sheath.

They are bloated, fat and cunning, and they're marvels as to size,
And their teeth can penetrate a sniping plate,
I could tell you tales unnumbered, but you'd think I', telling lies,
Of one old, grey whiskered buck-rat and his mate.

Just to show you, on my table lay a tin of sardines – sealed –
With the implement to open hanging near,
The old buck-rat espied them, to his missis loudly squealed,
"Bring quickly that tin-opener, Stinky dear!"

She fondly trotted up the pole, and brought him his desire,
He proceeded then with all his might and main,
He opened up that tin, and then – 'tis here you'll dub me "Liar!" –
He closed it down, and sealed it up again.

Have you seen one, should a rival chance to spoil his love affair,
Bring a bomb, Mills, hand, and place it underneath
The portion of the trench where that said rival had his lair,
And then he'll pull the pin out with his teeth.

He danced with rage, he howled and swore,
And vowed that he would see
That Army so contemptible
Would very quickly be
By every kind "of frightfulness"
Sent to eternity.

The Chancellor spoke loud and long,
With rhetoric inspired;
He spoke of love and peace and food,
He spoke till he was tired;
And when he paused he turned around ---
The War Lord had expired!

INTELLIGENCE
Summary measures

"O" the observer who stood at his post,
And at 3 on the 10th saw a small German host,
Going East with a cart, so he had a good look,
And proceeded to make – a note in his book.

"D" the Division who read the report the next day
The report "O" had rendered, and sent it away
To Corps where it rested, until bye and bye
The Army decided that those Huns should die.

So a mandate was issued ton Corps as a start,
To slaughter those Huns going East with a cart,
Which mandate was then with decision and case
Pushed on to Division, "for action please."

Division post-haste, or as near as could be,
Sent word to the gunners of what "O" could see,
The gunners prepared with shot and with shell,
To blow those said Germans from here into Hell.

With lanyard n hand, and with cool flashing eye,
They scanned all the landscape, they scanned all the sky –
And here we will leave them, gazing apart
For the Huns who – A WEEK AGO – passed with a cart.

****

Let me like a soldier fall,
Upon an open plain;
For if I trip and fall in a trench,
I could never get up again.

****

There was a little Hun, and at war he tried his hand,
And while that Hun was winning war was fine you understand,
But when the other hit him back he shouted in alarm,
A little drop of peace wouldn't do me any harm.

DISTURBING INFLUENCES

In dug-out cool I sit and freeze as on the war I ponder,
My thoughts on Huns and guns don't please, and so begin to wander,
Green fields, and peace, and lovely girls, or in my club I'm drinking,
When outside – bang – and of the war, I'm thinking, thinking, thinking.

I freely curse the blighted Hun who interrupts my fancies,
And with his frightfulness breaks in on memoried romances;
No Wilson I, nor has my pen much skill in temporisals,
So naught is left for me to do, save swift T.M. reprisals.

I hate all Huns, yet most hate I, that surly livered blighter,
Who with persistence breaks my sleep, with his ten times-a-nghter;
When fast asleep, and in the arms of Morpheus or some other,
The rotter looses off and then – oh damn it, there's another.

Yet will wait, and patiently, to catch the blighter bending,
And constantly unto my aid will summon guns unending;
With six-Inch Hows, and every kind of gun will wreck his dwelling,
And when we'll hold his requiem mass our Stokes shall do his knelling.

ONE

Gunners are a race apart,
Hard of head and hard of heart,
Like the gods they sit and view
All that other people do:
Like the Sister Three of Fate,
They do not discriminate.
Our support line, or the Hun's,
- What's the difference to the Guns?
Retaliation do you seek?
Ring them up, and – wait a week!
They will certainly reply
In the distant by –and-bye.
Should a shell explode amiss,
Each will swear it was not his:
For he never, never shot
Anywhere about that spot,
And, what's more, his Guns could not.

TWO

Sappers are wonderfully clever by birth,
And though they're not meek, they inherit the Earth.
Should your trenches prove leak, they'll work with a will
To make all the water flow up the next hill
(And when I say "work" I should really explain
That we find the Labour, while they find the Brain).
They build nice, deep dug-outs as quick as can be,
But quicker still mark them "RESERVED FOR R.E.":
And, strangely, this speed of theirs seems to decline
As the scene of their labours draws near the Front Line.

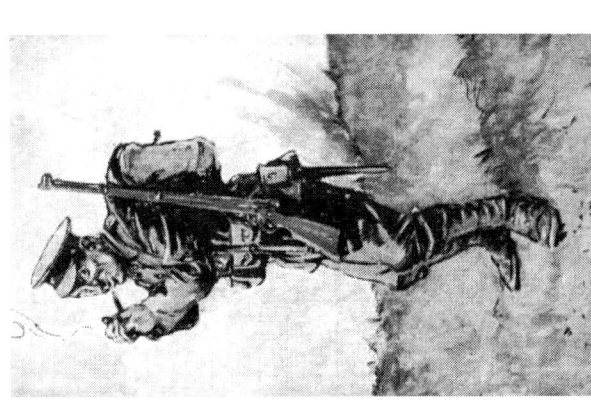

THE LEAVE WARRANT

Week, after weary week, I work and wait
Patiently wondering, when 'twill be my lot
To find a carpet, wond'rously wrought
On mystic looms, in some enchanted state,
Gifted with Oriental power innate
To bear me hence, to other lands, I wot
(In dreams, I sit upon it, but do not
Awake in time to ring the bell of fate)
But willingly, indeed, I would forego
This Magic Mat, for just a little bit
Of printed, primrose parchment – and to know,
That on its face my name three times was writ.
For 'tis a genie's golden key to fit
The Gate of Leave – "Chin chin, you chaps, cheer O!

C.L.P.

If I were King ! Ah! Bill, if I were King,
I wouldn' touch an "A" frame or a thing,
I'd watch the sergeant split his blooming thumb,
And, when he wasn't looking, drink his rum,
If I were King ! Ah! Bill, if I were King.

But I'm not King ! no Bill, I'm not the King,
So 'spose I've got to hump the blasted thing,
Gawd 'elp the 'un I get my 'ands upon,
One moment 'ere, and passing thence, 'e's gone,
'Tis soon we'll 'ave the blighter on a string.
"Gawd save the King, yus Bill! Gawd save the King."

THREE

Realising Men must laugh,
Some Wise Man devised the Staff:
Dressed them up in little dabs
Of rich variegated tabs:
Taught them how to win the war
On A.F.Z. 354:
Let them lead the simple life
Far from all our vulgar strife:
Nightly gave them downy beds
For their weary, aching heads:
Lest their relatives might grieve
Often, often, gave them leave,
Decorations, too, galore:
What on earth could man wish more?
Yet, alas, or so says Rumour,
He forgot a sense of Humour!

TO MELT A STONE

(letter from officer to his bank manager – with suitable alleged reply)

Kindly manager of Cox,
I am sadly on the rocks,
For a time my warring ceases,
My patella is in pieces;

Though in hospital I lie,
I am not about to die;
Therefore let me overdraw
Just a very little more,
If you stick to your red tape
I must go without my grape,
And my life must sadly fret
With a cheaper cigarette,
So pray be not hard upon
A poor dejected subaltern,
This is all I have to say,
"IMPECUNIOUS" R.F.A.

(ALLEDGED REPLY)

Sir, the kindly heart of Cox
Cannot leave you on the rocks,
And he should not sleep in bed
Thinking you were underfed;
So if you will let us know
Just how far you want to go,
Your request will not be vain,
Written from your bed of pain,
We will make but one request –
Keep this locked within your breast,
"Good old Cox is sure to pay,
For if other know, they'll say,
Only take him the right way."

(Note – this opens up new vistas. - Ed)

There was a little Turk, and Baghdad was his home,
There was a little Hun, and he lived in Bapaume,
Each said to the other, as they shivered with alarm,
"To find another home wouldn't do us any harm.

TEN GERMAN PIONEERS

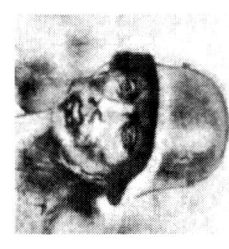

Ten German Pioneers went to lay a mine,
One dropped his cigarette, and then there were nine.
Nine German Pioneers singing hymns of hate,
One dropped a whiz-bang, and then there were eight.
Eight German Pioneers dreaming hard of Heaven,
One caught a Flying Pig, and then there were seven.
Seven German Pioneers working hard with picks,
One picked his neighbour off, and then there were six.
Six German Pioneers, glad to be alive,
One was sent to Verdun, and then there were five.
Five German Pioneers, didn't like the war,
One shouted "Kamarad" and then there were four.
Four German Pioneers fried to fell a tree,
One felled himself instead, and then there were three,
Three German Pioneers, prospects very blue,
One tried to stop a tank and then there were two.
Two German Pioneers walked into a gun,
The gunner pulled the lanyard, and then there was one.
One German Pioneer couldn't see the fun,
Of being shot at anymore, and so the war was done.

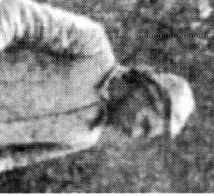

CONCERNING APOLOGIES
A Rhyme not without reason

"Only the wise apologise, Fools always must explain"
(Extract from a great modern poet)

On receipt of our verses, the Gunner grew pensive,
But quickly developed a counter offensive;
And through the rounds mostly were duds, or fell short,
They shewed themselves able to make some retort.

We all know the Sappers, of course, never shirk
From anything looking the least bit like WORK;
So pale, but determined, they swore, "He shall rue it!"
And asked for two large Working Parties to do it.

The Staff, though surprised, did not gibber or storm,
But dealt with it all on the Authorised Form;
For "D" said, "Well, I know whom that refers to,"
And passed the whole matter "for action" to "Q";
While "Q" patronisingly gave it a smile.
Remarked "Poor old 'G' Branch" and wrote on it "FILE"

P.B.!

THE SUB

He loves the Merry "Tatler," he adores the Saucy "Sketch,"
The "Bystander" also fills him with delight;
But the pages that he revels in, the evil, minded wretch,
Are the adverts of those things in pink and white.

They are advertised in crepe-de-chine, and trimmed with silk and lace;
The pictures fairly make him long for leave:
And while he gloats upon their frills, he cannot find the grace
To read the pars of PHRYNETTE, BLANCHE and EVE.

Before the war, he'd hardly heard of lave and lingerie;
He didn't know the meaning of chemise.
But thanks to weekly papers, this astounding mystery
Has been solved by dainty VENN and dear LABISE

Before the war, he only knew of corsets and of hats,
All other vogues invoked a ribald "what-ho."
But the last decree of Fashion is a dinky nightie, that's,
Embroidered with his regimental motto.

It's this war, that is responsible for teaching simple youth
All sorts of naughty Continental tricks.
And already he's decided, when its over, that, in truth,
He'll buy mamma a pair of cami-knicks.

SONG OF AN INFANTRY BRIDADIER TO HIS MEN

In my dug-out (where the plans are laid)
I sing this song to my Brigade.
You chaps who in a scrap have been
Will "compris" fully what I mean.
Just lately in the stunts you've struck,
You haven't had the best of luck.
You've had the kicks without the pence,
And always struck a stiffish fence.
You've had the mud: you've had the wet:
You've had the shells as well. An yet
You never grumble – just hold on
When all except your pluck has gone.
We know the cheery way you curse
When things are getting worse and worse,
Yet if I ask for further work,
There's not a dammed one here would shirk;
The Higher Staff quite understand,
But know the old Division, and
They know that they have but to ask,
And you will carry out the task.
So I have pledged my knightly word
To stick it out until the Third.
And though I pledge it with remorse
I pledge it hopefully; because
I know the stuff of which you're made,
I know the old "Umpteenth" Brigade.
I know you'll always play the game
(Although it is a b****y shame).
And so in tempest and in rain,
In shells and shells, and shells again,
Just understand (it's nothing new?)
How proud I am of all of you.

ROADS

Belgium, rain, and a sea of mud,
The first seven years are, they say, the worst;
The pave roads when you're spitting blood,
And all you have is a priceless thirst.

From Café Belge down to Kruistraathoek
In the same old rain, and the same old din;
From Hell Fire Corner to Bellewards Brook,
With the transport rattling on like sin.

We trod those roads in the days gone by
Till we knew each brick, or shell struck tree;
When the war was young, and our hopes ran high
That the summer would give us the victory.

Staggered along in the same old slush,
Dodging the crump=holes where one could;
Cursing all night, till the new dawn's blush
Found us just flitting from Zouave Wood.

Mush has been changed, but never the roads,
Each may be different yet each the same;
The same dammed pave, the same dammed loads,
And fewer return by the road we came.

Maybe one day we'll forget the rain,
The mud and the filth of a Belgian scene;
But always in mem'ry I'll see again
Those roads with stumps where the trees had been.

R.M.O.

IF THE RAIN AND THE WAR LAST

The summer had been long and cold,
And Intha Pink was growing old,
He stroked his hoary snow-white beard,
And gazed with eyes now long since bleared,
He scanned the waters deep and still,
And muttered grimly, "Swelp me, Bill.
Unless 'Aunt Sally' heaves in sight,
We'll get no rations up tonight!"

They steamed along at full six knots,
They dodged the shells, ignored the shots;
In fact the future seemed quite bright,
They'd get the rations there that night.

But stay, what means that sickening scrape,
That left them stranded and agape?
"her bottom's out!" old Intha cried,
And with a tin of biscuits tried
To stem the stream that flowed between
Her riven planks, but soon 'twas seen
That nothing now could put her right,
They'd get no rations up tonight.

'Twas now all hands to save them selves
On biscuit tins with pick-axe helves,
They rowed away, yet paused to find
The reason of their fate in kind ……
The waters, tired of rising higher,
Uncovered the Cathedral spire!
Uncharted, it had caused their plight,
No rations reached the line that night.

"She's late," he said in husky tones,
From near his feet came strangled moans,
He peered below into the gloom,
And for a sodden form made room,
'Twas Atkins of the P.B.I.,
Who brought the news that Hooge was dry,
And 'less they steered a half square right,
They'd get no rations up that night.

At last "Aunt Sally" hove in sight,
Old Intha hailed her with delight,
The rations soon were stowed inside,
And Atkins went to act as guide,

JIM

A hard little, scarred little terrier,
With a touch of the sheep-dog thrown in –
A mongrel – no matter,
There's no better ratter
In trenches or billet, than Jim.

A tough little, rough little beggar ;
And merry, the eyes of him.
But no Tarter or Turk
Can do dirtier work
With an enemy rat, than Jim.

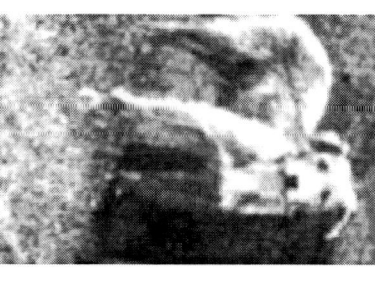

And when the light's done, and night's falling
And the shadows are darkling and dim,
In my ccat you will nuzzle
Your little pink muzzle
And growl in your dreams, little Jim.

R.M.O.

WHAT A HOPE

(From Captain Bingham Jones MC. to Colonel Spanker)

Dear Siree,

I have the honour to request,
That you will do your very best,
To recommend, and strongly too,
This my appeal I put to you,
To ask the G.O.C. if he,
His heart will soften, just for me,
My plea is nothing very mighty,
For four long months I've not been to Blighty,
If he a little leave will grant,
I'll go and see my wealthy aunt,
Who's lying on a bed of pain;
And never will get up again,
At least the doctor's say that's so,
And so I think I ought to go,
For if I don't I'm on the rocks,
The same applies to Messers Cox,
I therefore hope he will not choose,
My application to refuse,
And incidentally I'll add,
That when this "hoped for" leave I've had,
My work will please the C.R.E.,
As well as charm the G.O.C.
I have the honour, sir, to be,
Your humble servant, O.C. "D".

EXCELSIOR 1917

The shades of night were falling fast,
When up the muddy C.T. passed
A youth who bore, though looking glum,
A mighty gallon jar of rum.
    Excelsior!

"Try not to pass," the sergeant said,
"The blasted Hun might shoot you dead,
He's sniping near, he's shelling far,
Perhaps he'll hit that blooming jar!
    So leave it 'ere."

The youth moved on, no word spoke he
He wallowed up that old C.T.,
His visage grim showed pale in light
Where star shells glimmered through the night.
    Excelsior!

"Stay! Stay" my lad," the corp'ril cried,
"Another who the Hun defied
He got a bullet through the 'tum,'
And broke his blooming jar of rum,
    So go no more."

The youth's sad face showed grim and pale,
He struggled on into the gale,
Passed whiz-bangs urgent in their flight
Where bullets pinged through deepest night,
    And rain did pour.

"'Ere! Alfred, stop!" the private hailed,
The sad youth's face but paled and paled,
"Don't try that trench, the bloomin 'un
Is sweeping it with many a gun,
    'E'll 'it the jar."

"Ah stay me not," the youth replied,
"I must get there whate'er betide,
Though Hell may storm both near and far
I'll get there with this needed jar."
    He strode some more.

At last his goal appears in sight,
And blatant minnies rack the night,
He staggers to the Coy. H.Q.,
And to the precious jar he's true –
    He still it bore.

"Oh 'ell!" the sergeant raging stormed,
Then to the job in hand he warmed,
He told that youth who proudly bore
The jar through all! He told him more
    And more and more.

He told him all about his past,
His future, present, and at last
He paused for breath, he gasped and died,
And dying fell he down beside
    An empty jar.

WITH APOLOGIES TO RUDYARD KIPLING

When you're waiting for zero, to go o'er the top,
And yer mind gets a-wondering what you will stop,
Just go to yer bottle, and neck a wee drop,
Cos thinking' ain't good for a soldier.

When the 'un starts a barrage and you've nowhere to go,
Don't wander round looking for dugouts and so,
Just flop where you happen to be, don't you know
Any 'ole's good enough for a soldier.

When yer click for a leave, and yer warrant's come through,
Don't waste any time thinking what you will do,
Just grab up yer pack, leg it quick fer Berloo,
Any leave's good enough for a soldier.

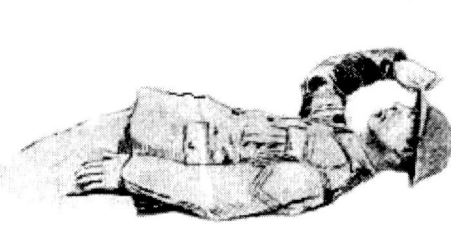

THE P.B.

I'm a twenty one years soldier, and I want to tell no lies,
But the job I'm now engaged on feeds me right up to the eyes.

Before the war in days of old, I ran a little show
Hawkin' rags and bones at Wigan, why I left it I don't know.

But I heard the bugles callin', and join up I felt I must,
Now I wish I'd let them bugles go on blowing' till they bust.

I joined to fight the Germans, and I crossed the angry sea,
Now I pick up bits of paper in a Depot, marked "P.B."

It's a bloomin' waste of money sendin' me across the foam
To pick up bits of paper, I could do that job at home.

And the soldiers think it funny, that's what fills my bitter cup,
For they chuck down bits of paper just to see me pick 'em up.

They keep me in the Depot, 'cause I've got a nasty wheeze,
D.A.H., and bad bronchitis, and I'm groggy at the knees.

I tried to get some home leave I did, I said my wife was dead,
They found I'd never had a wife, and I got crimed instead.

I tried to go to Orspital, I showed a wobbly knee,
I got what I expected, number 9, and M and D.

Last week they had a paper chase, and all the Depots went;
I had to follow up the 'ounds, and gather up the scent.

On windy days they form a ring, and make a horse of me,
And back their bits of paper, ten to one against P.B.

Once by mistake I found myself included in a draft,
The things that happened in the line have fairly turned me daft.

I joined a working party going on up to the line,
The Hun he started shelling, so I thought I'd do a shine.

I crawled into a drain-pipe to hide me from the Hun:
Then someone cried "Get out you fool, you're in a twelve-inch gun!"

I got back home – I don't know how – and saw the Batt M.O.,
He passed me back again P.B., to where the sea winds blow.

So here I am and here I'll stop; I'm bound to see it through,
I'll pick up bits of paper if my Country wants me to.

H.H.W.

SEEN FROM AN AID-POST

There are many roads in Flanders, where the horses slide and fall,
There are roads of mud and pave, that lead nowhere at all,
They are roads, that finish in a trench; the Germans hold the rest.
But of all the roads in Flanders, there is one I know the best.
It's a great road, a straight road, a road that runs between
Two rows of broken poplars, that were young and strong and green.

You can trace it from old Poperinghe, through Vlamertinghe and Wipers;
(It's a focus for Hun whiz-bangs and a paradise for snipers)
Pass the solid Ramparts, and the muddy moat you're then in,
The road I want to sing about – the road that leads to Menin.
It's a great road, a straight road, a road that runs between
Two rows of broken poplars, that were young and strong and green.

It's a road that's cursed by smokers; for you dare not show a light;
It's a road, that's shunned by daytime; and is mainly used by night,
Bu at dusk the silent troops come up, and limbers bring their loads
Of ammunition to the guns, that guard the Salient's roads.
It's a great road, a straight road, a road that runs between
Two rows of broken poplars, that were young and strong and green.

And for hours and days together, I have listened to the sound
Of German shrapnel overhead, while I was underground
In a damp and cheerless cellar, continually trying
To dress the wounded warriors, while comforting the dying
On that muddy road, that bloody road, that road that runs between
Two rows of broken poplars, that were young and strong and green.

R.M.O.

Untitled

Sentry! What of the night?
The sentry's answer I will not repeat,
Though short in words, 'twas with feeling replete,
It covered all he thought and more,
It covered all he'd thought before,
It covered all he might think yet
In years to come. For he was wet
And had no rum.

Untitled

Walking one day on a duckboard
I was weary and ill at ease,
And my hands grasped vainly at nothing,
And the mud came up to my knees,
The duckboard began oscillating,
I knew that I had to go,
So I gave one wild and final plunge,
And fell in the mud below.

Untitled

Sing a song of Christmas!
Pockets full of slush,
Four and twenty P.B.I.
A dixey full of "mush,"
When the dixey opened
The Tommies said "Oh my!
It's beef to-day by way of change"
And then began to cry.

THE BURNING QUESTION

Three tommies sat in a trench one day,
Discussing the war, in the usual way,
They talked of the mud, and they talked of the Hun,
Of what was to do, and what had been done,
They talked about rum, and – 'tis hard to believe –
They even found time to speak about leave,
But the point which they argued from post back to pillar
Was whether Notts County could beat Aston Villa.

The Earth shook and swayed, and the barrage was on
As they leapt o'er the top with a rush, and were gone
Away into Hunland, through mud and through wire,
Stabbing and dragging themselves through the mire,
No time to heed those who are falling en route
Till, stopped by a strong point, they lay down to shoot,
Then through the din came a voice; "Say, Jack Miller!
I tell yer Notts County can beat Aston Villa"

The strong point had gone, and forward they press
Towards their objective, in number grown less
They reach it at last, and prepare to resist
The counter-attack which will come through the mist
Of the rain falling steadily;
Dig and hang on,
The word for support back to H.Q. has gone,
The air, charged with moment, grows stiller and stiller –
"Notts County's no earthly beside Aston Villa."

Two "Blighties," a struggle through mud to get back
To the old A.D.S. down a rough duck-board track,
A hasty field dressing, a ride in a car,
A wait in a C.C.S., then there they are:
Packed side by side n a clean Red Cross train,
Happy in hopes to see Blighty again,
Still, through the bandages, muffled, "Jack Miller",
I bet Notts Couty can beat Aston Villa!"

The night sped away, and zero drew nigh,
Equipment made ready, all lips getting dry,
And watches consulted with each passing minute
Till five more to go, then 'twould find them all in it;
The word came along down the line to "get ready!"
The sergeants admonishing all to keep steady,
But out rang a voice getting shriller and shriller;
"I tell yer Notts County can beat Aston Villa!"

WITH THE USUAL APOLOGIES (to IF)

If you can drink the beer the Belgians sell you,
And pay the price they ask with ne'er a grouse,
If you believe the tales that some will tell you,
And live in mud with ground sheet for a house,
If you can live on Bully and a biscuit,
And thank you stars that you've a tot of rum,
Dodge whiz-bangs with a grin, and as you risk it
Talk glibly of the pretty way they hum,
If you can flounder through a C.T. nightly
That's three-parts full of mud and filth and slime,
Bite back the oaths and keep your jaw shut tightly,
While inwardly you're cursing all the time,
If you can crawl through wire and crump holes reeking
With feet of liquid mud, and keep your head
Turned always to the place which you are seeking,
Through dread of crying you will laugh instead,
If you can fight a week in Hell's own image,
And at the end just throw you down and grin,
When every bone you've got starts on a scrimmage,
And for a sleep you'd sell your soul within,
If you can clamber up with pick and shovel,
And turn your filthy crump hole to a trench,
When all inside you makes you itch to grovel,
And all you've had to feed on is a stench,
If you can hang on just because you're thinking
You haven't got one chance in ten to live,
You will see it through, no use in blinking
And you're not going to take more than you give,
If you can grin at last when handing over,
And finish well what you had well begun,
And think a muddy ditch a bed of clover,
You'll be a soldier on day, then, my son.

WHY NOT

We've had a play in ragtime, and we've had a ragtime band,
We've had a ragtime army, and we've had a ragtime land;
But why not let us have what we have never had before?
Let's wade right in tomorrow and let's have a ragtime war.

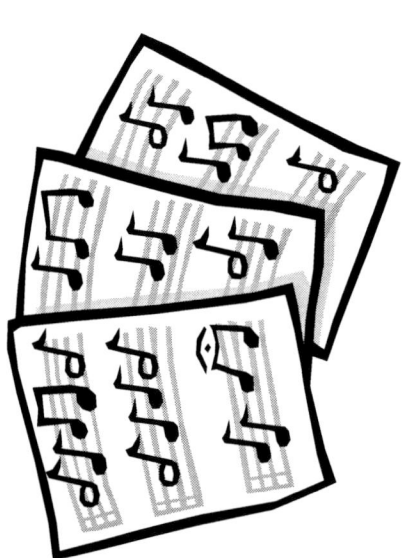

Let's carry up our duck-boards to a ragtime's jerky strains,
Let's whistle ragtime ditties while we're bashing out Hun brains,
Let's introduce this melody in all we say and do,
In our operation orders, and in all our lies to Q.

Let us write O.O.'s to music, and the red-hats can decide
The witching hour of zero to a dainty Gaby Glide,
We'll take the fateful plunge, and when we venture o'er the top,
We'll do it to a Turkey Trot or tuneful Boston Hop.

We'll drink our S.R.D. to tune, and even "chatting up"
Becomes a melody in rhyme if done to "Dixie Pup,"
A bombing raid to "Old Kentuck" would make a Fritzie smile,
He'd stop a bomb with pleasure to a ragtime's mystic guile.

Can you see our giddy "Q" staff, as they go up to the line,
Just walking round the trenches to the air "Kentucky Mine,"
Gaily prancing down the duckboards, as they tumble o'er a bucket,
To the quiet seducing strains of "My Dear Home in Old Kentucket."

THOUGHTS

I aint no blooming Kipling, and I ne'er could be a Keats,
But I somehow sees a poem in what'er I drinks and eats;
When the night has fallen round me lovely verses seem to come,
As my thoughts in fancy linger on my evening tot of rum.

Oh! Naught in Heaven's pellucid heights
When shadows play in Very Lights,
Can stem the fervent words which come
When'er the sergeant drinks our rum.

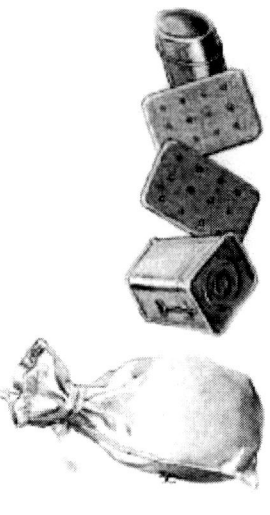

There's a poem in a biscuit, there's a poem in our tea,
In fact the blooming rations make a book of poetry;
But to have the gift to find it and to understand it fully,
One must learn to look for Khayyar in a blooming tin of bully.
For all the wine you drink, the lips you press,
Will only land you in some blooming mess,
And fourteen days F.P. No.1;
But bully's bully, neither more or less.

You can have your blooming Shelly,
Browning too, what did they know?
They could only see a poem in the way the daisies grow;
Had I got five francs to bet 'em then I'd very quickly risk it
That they couldn't find a poem in a blooming Army biscuit.

Hard is my lot, and hard is the world,
Hard are the shells day and night at us hurled,
Hard is the pave, and hard is the stone,
But for hardness the biscuit's a class on its own.

A WAIL

Life has many disappointments,
Days are never free from care,
For in spite of using ointments
Steadily I'm losing my hair.

PROFIT AND LOSS

Now William Hohenzollern, the King of all the Huns,
Had quite a lot of country and he also had six sons,
Of money too he'd plenty and a larder fully stocked-
In fact he'd all he wanted – so at grief and care he mocked.

Karl Baumberg lived in comfort with his frau and family,
His sons they numbered seven, and his daughters numbered three;
They'd just enough of everything and wished for nothing more,
(This happy time, you understand, was just before the war).

For reasons which they never knew Karl Baumberg's seven sons
Were quickly clad in suits of grey and labelled "food for guns,"
Two rot in mud near Wipers, and another at Verdun,
The Somme accounted for a brace, and Passchendaele for one.

The one remaining to old Karl is minus both his arms,
His fighting days are finished, and he's sick of war's alarms;
He grinds his teeth with fury, while old Karl hunts round for food,
And his mother freely curses both the Kaiser and his brood.

His one remaining sister (death has claimed the other two)
Out of water and a horse bone tries to make a dish of stew,
Comes a mandate "Our great Kaiser has another victory won
Fly your flags and cheer, by order, for the victory of Verdun."

Then old Karl, whose waking senses grasp a fact both strange and new,
That the victories are worthless if they bring no end in view,
And he curses Kaiser William who's the King of all the Huns,
But his frau is quietly sobbing for – the Kaiser has six sons.

ANOTHER WAIL

Oh Mr. Cox! Oh Mr. Cox!
My heart you've nearly broken,
By telling me I'm on the rocks
In words most harshly spoken.

You say that I have overdrawn
A sum quite awe-inspiring,
If that were all I would not mourn,
Nor would I be perspiring.

But to these awful words you add
A legend disconcerting,
In large black print, which makes me sad,
My tender feelings hurting.

Your envelope, in words of fire,
Inscribed, "Buy War Bonds NOW!"
My dear old Cox just send a wire
And tell me, tell me, HOW?

BILL SHAKESPEARE

STICK IT

What matter though the wily Hun
With bomb, and gas and many a gun
In futile fury, lashes out,
Don't wonder what it's all about –
    "Stick it."

When soaked n mud, half dead with cold,
You curse that you're a soldier bold;
Don't heave you "A" frame through the night,
And, though it's wanted, travel light –
    "Stick it."

Although it always seems your fate
To join a working party, mate
Don't curse the sergeant, 'taint his show,
The work's to do, just grin and so –
    "Stick it."

Though Belgium beer seems poor and thin,
And leaks the billet you are in;
When you are resting, some parade
Bursts all the lovely plans you've made –
    "Stick it."

Though shelled by day and bombed at night,
A shirt, though lively, dry, delight
When half-way there, you think your back
Must break, you're thirsty, grub you lack –
    "Stick it."

As someone said, there's no road yet
But had an end, your grinders set
On this one thing, that if you grin
And carry on, we're sure to win –
    "Stick it."

SOME HAVE FAME THRUST UPON THEM

–Twas a sentry young on a lonely post
And he scanned the earth and sky,
When he was aware of a red tapped throng
Which came a-trotting by.

Now the leading wight was a general old,
And the rest, some far, some nigh,
Came panting on in the deuce of a sweat;
The sentry wondered why.

But the general stopped and he spake these words,
"So you watch the earth and sky!
Do you know that the fate of an empire hangs
On just *your* watchful eye"

'Twas a grubby fist that the general grasped
"You'll be proud lad by and bye,
That you shook my hand on a summers day;
Your Corps Commander I.

When the sentry left to his lonely post,
He winked at the earth and sky,
Far off in the trenches a mile away,
Faint streaks of red flashed by.

THE FIFTH AND LAST

In 14 when the war was young
By military ardour stung
We'd donned the khaki, and begun
To train for smashing up the Hun ;
Our tutors, though assuming lore
And dishing out wild tales of gore,
Knew just as much of war as we –
Which was *narpoo, you must compree.*

At 6a.m. each winter's morn
The Front at Brighton looked forlorn
Yet not one tenth forlorn as we,
Who willy-nilly did P.T.
With mingled curses, sobs and groans
We dislocated all our bones,
Yet suffered gladly all that tosh
Thinking I twould help to smash the "boche."

Our next Noel was passed in France,
At war by then we looked askance,
We'd sampled some of it at Loos
And for it's charms had little use;
We'd tried St Eloi and The Bluff
And thought the Huns uncouth and rough,
Yet things all panned out for the best
That Xmas Day found us "at rest."

The Natal Day of 16 found
Us back at Loos, the same old round
Of trenches, minnies, shells and mud,
Lord! How we'd got to hate the thud
Of shrieking hunks of metal, which
Just passed your ear and struck your ditch,
And to us all just then it seemed
This was not war of which we'd dreamed.

Another twelve months rolled away
Each month a year, each hour a day,
A Plethora of blood and woe
The net result "in statu quo";
That Christmas Day itself we'd got
The soldiers dream – a cushy spot,
St Quentin just in front you'd find
The same old Somme battlefield behind.

By then we'd given up surmise
When peace would come and in what guise,
Nor wondered if it were to last
Noel which was at war be passed
Just spared some breath to curse the Hun
For all he did, for all he'd done,
For all he yet might do, *après*
We'd celebrate our Christmas Day.

And now we've reached the last Noel
The job completely done and well,
We've done with mud and shells and stench,
Hope ne'er again to see a trench,
No more to hear the crumps come in,
The whizzbang's shriek, the minnies din,
The long last years have been well worth
If once again we've "Peace on Earth."

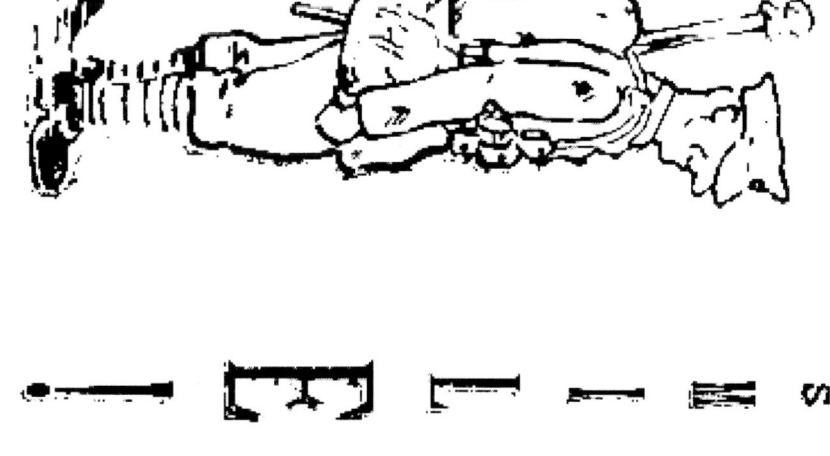

THE DEMOBILISATION

PEACE

'Twas nice while it lasted, we needed the more
Of living in harmony with one another,
Rather than suffering the effects of the war,
Why? oh why? will you not call me "brother."

C.H.

1939 WAR AGAIN

The Second World War began in 1939 and was to last until 1945. It was fought in many theatres of war and against more than one foe. This was not a static war as that of 1914-18 had been and we do not see poetry being written in the same volume. However, we do have poetry from those who had been taken Prisoners of War, possibly because they had the time to sit and muse.

The first nine poems in this section, were all written by Private Charles H. Raybould, who served with the 14th Battalion, The Sherwood Foresters

Ireland

Bloodstained hands,
Stain Erin's troubled land,
Tyrannical in long revolts,
Sparked by religious ire.

Snigger sly, garrulous I.R.A. guns.
Deaths kicking thunder-bolts,
Explosive lunatics desire.
Day by, nightmare, bullets, bombs, frightening day.
Bears shoulder high- Provender.

Another, yet another and another,
English, Irish funeral bier,
Irelands bitter cup of Woe.
Now, their only World of Peace.
Nights opiate of sleep.

A fitful,
Spiteful pause.
Quiescent under nocturnal twitching stars,
Evanescing with,
Waking daylights shattering applause.

Four Derbyshire Infantrymen In a Desert Trench at El-Alamein

Four Derbyshire infantrymen
Talked in a stove-hot trench.
Three thousand odd miles from home,
Sweltering in Africa's noon-day sun.
Desert tanned,
Four Derbyshire infantrymen, let their minds roam.

War less…haversacked…free…
Four happy, virile, young men climbed, kinderscout,
Suspended in mid air,
Heedless of their Platoon Sergeants warning shout,
Three thousand miles from home.
In a fly-infested trench, lizards frolicked,

As four Derbyshire infantrymen
Talked and walked, reminiscing,
Then hungry, halted.
Hands gathering Hathersages fat Septembers blackberries,
Before the autumn sun,
Began closing his benediction.

As deserts burning wind, orchestras played sobbing violins,
With English skylarks throating their full requiems,
Three thousand miles from home.
Then a German shell, in wars anger screamed.
Deaths destructive avalanche?
Silencing four Derbyshire men's infantrymen's conversation.

Sleeping their unwearied sleep,
Regimented lines and spaces,
Side by side, with death.
That un-chosen, that indelible,
That unwanted mate!

Lest We Forget
From a British War Cemetery in North Africa

Confined,
Chilled penury.
The grave's bitter,
Claustrophobic penitentiary.
Ungoverned,
Uncommunicative,
Death's prisoners.

Montgomery's desert rats,
Hanks of shredded hair,
Bleached, unrobed bones.
Soldiers shorn of militant armoury.
Divorced.
Dusts deaf ears
From wars and litany.

It's sudden demise,
Executing life's swift release,
For this vast,
Invisible, mute, supine,
Ambitionless, brave audience.

War's grim, chronicled trophies.
Britons, foreign lodgers laid,
In sands mercurial,
Memorial, sepulchral,
Death's shade.

Cathedral quiet,
Until, Africa's noon days toast,
Hot winds,
Orchestras play,
A deserts haunting violins,
Over young men's joyless fate,
Ageless.

In Action *Normandy*

The stammering dialogue of bren,
The cough, cough, cough
Of trench ensconced, Private Chalky White.
A sick war-weary, rain soaked, miserable man.
Fluorescent lit,
By ascending enemy very-light flare.
Fireworks igniting Normandy's heavens.

Dawn's broadcasts,
Earshot caught.
A larks frail unpublished symphony,
Playing to nigger-night's dying stars.
The desultory sigh,
And thump of shell-fire,
Imitating a N.C.O.'s authoritative voice.

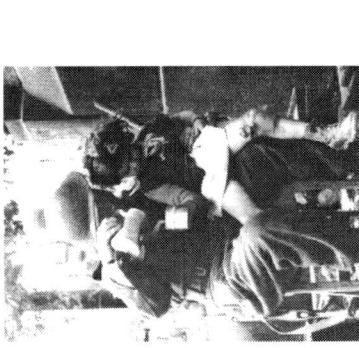

"Stretcher bearers?"
"A badly wounded man over here."
Then,
A cathedral hush,
As war's lunatic rage is momentarily suspended.
A Green Howard's wag cracked,
"Hey, lads,
This bloody stupid war's ended."

Zero Hour Somewhere in *Normandy*

Bad luck!
A bakers dozen spring birds
Arrowed low overhead.
A war-less chain…
Tiny flesh and feathers.
Dawns first lark, drunkenly rose
From its rain-soaked French bed,
As though puppet manipulated,
On invisible thread.
Yo-yo operating,
Short bursts,
Ascending,
Descending,
Ascending.

Frail musical-downy throat,
Exquisitely serenading.
It ironically seemed,
A pre-arranged signal.
For spooky first-lights advance,
After a two hour breather.
Stupified,
Dew-wet,
Malarial shivering,
With addled brains,
Throning lunacy's bulging eyes.
Woken from a brief nap snatched.
Infantrymen zig-zag ran,
Some comically clown falling.
Some stumbling,
sprawling,
Rigor mortis
twitching.
Death obscene,
Prostrate,
On April's rice pudding ground.

Rear-Guard Action
From Le-Mans Down to St.Nazaire Harbour, June 1940

Death's journeying.
Grey, painting each suntanned soldier's face,
Wearing slack, opened mouths.
Idiot, old man gaping.
Expressionless young men's
Fixed lined eyes,
Heavenwards staring.
All dead infantrymen.
Two of 'em,
My best mates,
Bloody heart-breaking.

Corpses

"Wakey, wakey"
Shouted us marching,
Odds and sods,
From lost, split up mobs.
Passing khaki islands,
Of untidy, sprawling war-stained young men,
Laying silent, unflinching.
As German planes screamed overhead.
A machine gun typewriter clattered.
Didn't disturb the infantrymen.
If this platoon of Sherwood Foresters had been alive,
They would have leapt up and hid.

Lest We Forget
'C' Company, Sherwood Foresters Resting in a Normandy Orchard, May 1940

Normandy's orchard apple blossoms,
Riots of war-less scented arms.
Flowering umbrellas,
Shading young Sherwood Forester's,
War-wearied bones.

Some alive, in tense suspense,
Every name I could mention.
Some dead,
Supine, suntanned young limbs,
Almost to attention.

With khaki arms,
East and West extended.
England's blossoms,
Soldier's crosses,
France's permanent lodgers.

Their hostilities ended,
Their life's ambitions dead.
Barren, their thought-less days,
Grievous their losses.

Circumscribed beneath stone tides,
Chronicling-
Numbers, ranks, names, Regiments,
Embossed on marble crosses,
Regimented lines on parade.

Cenotaph

Whitehall- based,
Transfixed,
Monumental,
Joyless,
Marble,
Immemorial grey ghost.

A forget-me-not,
When massed bugles cry.
That trembling,
That sou -reaching,
That haunting, Last Post.

Pregnant with grief,
Moving strong, ex-fighting men,
To moist eye.
Seeing in each Remembrance Day's poppy,
Staring their mourning power.
A slain man's tragic face,
Framed in each blood-red artificial flower.

The remaining poems are all believed to have been written By Prisoner's of War. He majority are unsigned but where possible, credit is given to the poet. All the following poems were found in the papers of 4978755 Private Lawrence Wheatley and are all unsigned – we can only assume that he wrote a number of them.

Egypt

Land of sweat and sweaty paws,
Sand storms, flies, and desert sores,
Streets of sorrow, streets of shame,
Streets of which I give no name,
Streets of filth, and stinking dogs,
Harlots, thieves, and stinking wogs.

Clouds of dust that choke and blind,
Drives us fellows from our mind,
Aching hearts and aching feet,
Gyppo guts and camel meat,
Arabs Heaven, soldiers Hell,
Land of Pharaohs,
"Fare thee well."

Dearest

Dearest one in all the world,
I think of you today.
But when I come to tell my thoughts,
I know not what to say,
For words are clumsy things at best,
And hearts are slow to yield,
To the deep and tender secrets,
In their silent depths concealed.
But when I call you dearest,
That word seems to convey,
The story of my love for you,
And though you're far away,
It grows stronger as time passes,

Ever constant, ever true.
Dearest and most precious one,
My heart belongs to <u>YOU</u>.

Untitled

There's so much good in the worst of us,
And so much bad in the best of us,
That it does not pay either one of us,
To find fault with the rest of us.

Safe Keeping

I pray for your safe keeping,
With every hour that chimes,
Through all the pains and perils,
And terrors of the times.

We cannot be together,
These troubled days to share,
But may you be protected,
This is my constant prayer.

That you be delivered,
Through all the strife and strain,
God have you in his keeping,
Until we meet again.

Faithful

I've tried a hundred million times,
To write a bunch of funny rhymes,
To bring you joy instead of tears,
In case these months grow into years.
But all my efforts went for nought,
My heart excludes all comic thought.
The ache in it that your absence brings,
Keeps tugging wildly at the strings,
And keeps me lonesome all the while,
Until your letters reconcile.

So looking forward to the times,
Our happiness will be sublime.
I send my love to let you know,
That I am yours wher'er I go,
And hope each melancholy day,
Will quickly dawn and slip away,
Till we are back as once before,
Just you and I and nothing more,
Except our love and all our dreams,
Which had to wait for grimmer schemes.

My thoughts are ever with you,
Although we are apart,
In daytime and in darkness,
You're always in my heart.

Men England Forgot

Out here in the desert, the hot blazing sun,
Beats down on the heads of Tommy and Hun.
The "Africa Corps." is the name of one lot,
The name of the other, "Men England forgot."

We think of old England, the joys and the fun,
We enjoyed so immensely when day's work was done.
Yes! We think of old England, who thinks of us not,
But we'll always remember, "Men England forgot."

Despite flies and sandstorms, and blistering heat,
We plod through the desert on hot aching feet,
Though tired and weary and ready to drop,
You can't beat those heroes, "Men England forgot."

You've heard of Cairo, and nights on the spree,
Of Alex and wonderful days by the sea,
But you've never heard tell of the filth and rot,
That was borne by those outcasts, "Men England forgot."

And when it's all over, and we're safe at home,
We'll think of the days that we spent o'er the foam,
Yes! We'll think of the sand, and the blazing hot,
And we will always remember, "Men England forgot."

The Call to Home

Others are waiting as well as you,
To hear the last all clear,
For time is drawing so close to,
Who knows! Maybe this year.

They lived and strived and toiled,
For the voice of man to sing,
It's message to this waiting world,
That the bells of peace will ring.

The echo of those wondrous chimes,
Will fill their hearts with joy,
For once again to have those times,
As they did in days gone by.

And when they know their term is done,
They'll long for their one hope,
It's in the mind of everyone,
Yes, roll on that boat.

Out of the Blue

The city throbs with the pulse of life,
With commerce and industry ever at strife,
With hustle and bustle and traffics roar,
Far from the sounds of distant war.
The parks are all dressed in their floral gown,
And peace prevails in the old home towns,
The big bombs that roar, and the sirens that moan,
Are things, thank God, which are quite unknown.

But way out here in the distant blue,
There's a living hell, that men go through,
As day by day, and night by night,
They are locked in the grip of the world's worst fight.
As courageously striving, they stagger and reel,
To ward off the menacing Nazi heel,
To spare their loved ones, they left behind,
From the rope of bondage, the foe had in mind.

Yet down in the city, seek and you'll find,
Men who have chosen to stay on behind,
Watching the fight on a silvery screen,
Sipping their whiskies, calm and serene.
Reading the paper, discussing the news,
Laughing and joking, and airing their views,
Sleeping each night in a cosy bed,
While their fellow men crash to the desert, stone dead.

Out in the desert, clouded in sand,
Death swings his scythe with an unerring hand,
Reaping the harvest so bloody and grim,
Which Germany, long, long ago, promised him.
That harvest of youth on the threshold of life,
All trapped in the grip of a Titan strife,
Your husbands, sweethearts and also your sons,
Gallantly fighting and manning the guns.

Yet down in the city, if you care, you'll find,
Men who have chosen to stay on behind,
When they do sport each weekend in white flannel pants,
And a cinema show, then maybe a dance.
At which, holding you close in un-uniformed arms,
They whisper banalities, talk of their charms,
Speak of their love, and their love for you,
As long as it keeps them <u>out of the blue.</u>

While borne on the crest of a ghostly tide,
Death goes around with his arrogant stride,
Whispering the name of someone you love,
While Stuka's scream down from the heavens above.
To shower their bombs with murderous aim,
On the men they've been sent out to kill or maim,
Leaving them lying in a dark pall of smoke,
To bleed, to cry out, to die and to choke.

Still in the city, should you seek, you'll find,
Those men who have chosen to stay home behind,
Stout hearted fellows with hearts of pure gold,
Gold that is yellow or so we are told.
Eager to share in the peace victory brings,
Claiming the rights to life's precious things,
Proud of the fact that they'd nothing to lose,
Theirs was the choice and they knew what to choose.

When the battle is over and victory won,
When the hell with its carnage and gunfire is done,
When homeward they march, those fortunate few,
To pick up the threads of life they once did knew.
How will they know as they march down the street,
Which echoes the tramp of their military feet,
That the value they placed on their homeland with you,
Was settled and paid for out there in the blue.

Settled and paid for without any doubt,
By they and their comrades who proudly set out,
Who suffered agonies, torture and pain,
Of the war in the desert and tropical plain.
Who gamely and doggedly, stuck it and won,
To prove to the world and the God up above,
That it's you above all on this earth that they loved.
Still down in the city, seek and you'll find,
Curs who have chosen to stay home behind.

One is my Mother

A group of soldiers, one night in their camp,
Were talking of sweethearts they had,
Excepting one fellow, who held down his head,
He was looking downhearted and sad.
"Come and join us", said one of the boys,
Surely someone loves you so,
He held up his head,
And proudly he said, "Boys, I'm in love with two."

One has hair of silvery grey,
The other has hair of gold,
One is young and beautiful,
The other is bent and old,
Those are the two that are dear to me,
From them I never will part,
For one is my mother, God bless her, I love her,
And the other is my sweetheart.

My sweetheart, she's only a plain working girl,
And to her I hope to be wed,
But Father says "No! It cannot be so."
"You must marry a Lady instead."
I go to my mother, she knows how things are,
When Father wed her she was poor,
"Cheer up and don't fret, she'll be your wife yet,
And with Father's consent I am sure."

The bells are ringing for me and my gal,
The world is singing for me and my gal,
Everybody is knowing, to a wedding they're going,
And for weeks they've been sewing, every Suesy and Sal,
Their congratulations for me and my gal,
And someday we'll build a cosy little nest,
For two or three or four or more,
In love land for me and my gal.

Kiss the boys goodbye

Daddy may I stay out late,
For tomorrow is my wedding date,
Can't your baby kinda celebrate,
And kiss the boys goodbye.

Daddy may I wear the mink,
What's the difference what the neighbours think,
Let your baby linger on the brink,
And kiss the boys goodbye.

While I'm kissing them sentimentally,
Keep the liberal point of view,
Because I'm breaking it to them gently,
But my heart belongs to you.

Daddy please remember this,
That tomorrow starts a life of bliss,
So let me show them what they're going to miss,
And kiss the boys goodbye.

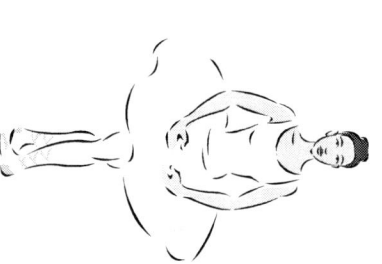

Birthday Greetings to my Lady

So my dear! Once more you stand at the gateway,
Of yet another year, your life speeding away,
You'll never know the depth of longing in me,
To taste afresh with you the joys that once we knew,
Joyfully, memory recalls those happy, golden hours,
To me, in loneliness, they are fragrant as God's flowers.

They are parts of happy days,
Memory brings them back again,
Oh such pleasure, such pain,
Hills and dales, country walks and rippling streams,
Each scene, each resting place, now glows and gleams,
Richly coloured by the rainbow tints of memory,
Who could, who would, forget the heartache, the bliss?

They made our happy days,
For love's sweet sake, they must come back again.
Oh! Delightful pleasure, transfiguring pain,
Once again "My dear", 'tis your birthday,
Your lover far away,
In language which only lovers know,
The old sweet things we say.

But for today, God bless and keep you, I pray,
I know that we are in his hands,
Wherever we are,
Knowing this, to you I shall come though from afar.

Never Forget

Never forget how much I love you,
Never forget how much I care,
Always my loving arms are waiting,
With you everything I long to share,
God will send a fair tomorrow,
And when he sends that perfect day,
We'll forget we had to part dear,
And that I had to go away.

Oh! But to look on the moors and hills,
Purple beneath the sun,
Oh! But to wander by old, old paths,
In the peace of a day that is done,
Cherished the dream of a heart once young,
Dreams we can never forget,
Wide is the sea, but ere will be,
The love of the hearts that wait.

Red Cross Parcel Day

'Twas in an old stalag,
Where my friend would sit and sigh,
Waiting for the hour,
When parcel day comes nigh.
But as he'd sit and wonder,
Of the days he had done stag,
No thought of any parcel,
Each week he would ever have.

His only thought was work and pay,
And hearing someone say, "Get weaving",
But now, today is parcel day,
And he was a parcel given,
So now he's filled with rapture,
And carried away to Heaven,
To think that all those lovely things,
Should come just through his capture.

You'll see he gets some better meals,
And feels proud we have Red Cross,
For now he's making an appeal,
For all to help them in the cause.
So if you see the crimson cross,
Just give a think to all the cost,
To make that lad of yours.
A happy P.O.W.

(Signed) **Lawrence Wheatley**

Waiting

When you're far away from the one you love,
Stop and gaze at the Heavens above,
Whether the time be the sun-scorched noon,
Or a frosty night, with a glittering moon.

And there up above in that realm of space,
I see not the sun or moon, but a face,
A beautiful face, with a tender smile,
Which tells me she's waiting to make life worthwhile.

Perhaps tonight from her window pane,
She's gazing aloft, on her lips my name,
As she prays to God, way up above,
To watch over, keep safe, and return that love.

So when you're feeling alone and forlorn,
Watch into the night and the wakening morn,
And remember that westward across the blue,
She's watching, and waiting, the same as you.

Anon.
Signed **"By a P.O.W."**

The final flurry of poems are (unless otherwise shown) all from the pen of 4979727 Lance Corporal Fred Jeffery, who served with the 2/5th Battalion

War

Did you ever spare a thought,
For many of the men that fought,
Theirs was a sad and sorry fate,
Imprisoned in a land of hate.
For many days to wait and yearn,
Hoping that soon they will return.
How did they pass their time away?
What did they think from day to day?
How did they hide their misery?
Just read within and you will see.

By Jock Ingram, Prisoner of War (2nd World War).

P.O.W

Barren wastes of scrub and sand,
Dry desert land,
Spiked wire on every hand.
Prisoners of War.

A hopeless host of hungry men,
Crowded like rats in cage and pen,
Shut off, it seems from human ken.
Prisoners of War.

Ill clad, unkempt and under-fed,
Trading their watches and ring for bread,
A chill and concrete floor their bed.
Prisoners of War.

Queuing for hours in blistering heat,
Receiving a morsel of bread and meat,
Glad of even the scraps to eat.
Prisoners of War.

Bullied and driven, like flocks of sheep,
Treated like dirt from dawn till sleep,
Hearts being filled with a hatred deep.
Prisoners of War.

Cut off from news from the outside world,
Sifting the truth from the taunts that are hurled,
Silently keeping the flag unfurled.
Prisoners of War.

Striving to keep alive your hope,
Feeling at times it's beyond your scope,
Drugging yourself with rumour as dope.
Prisoners of War.

Setting new value to trivial things,
The smell of a flower, a skylark that sings,
The beauty and grace of a butterfly's wings.
Prisoners of War.

Learning that life without freedom is in vain,
'Tis better to die than live ever in pain,
Thank God for some hope of release once again.
Prisoners of War.

Seeing new meaning in higher things,
In life, in Christ, in the hope he brings,
Thus did they treat the King of Kings.
Prisoners of War.

Finding at last if you've eyes to see,
This glorious truth, fixed by God's decree,
As long as the soul is unchanged, you're free.
Prisoners of War.

P.O.W. Life

Have you ever been in a prison camp,
Beneath the Italian skies?
Where the food and drink make a man think
That Hell is a real paradise.

Where the gay caballero's with their toothpick swords,
And hats like a large Christmas pud,
Travel around with their nose to the ground,
Like some of Walt Disney's brood.

Where your measly pay is a lire a day,
And cigs you get when they come,
Where the prisoner's latrines are never kept clean,
For they stink, they smell and they hum.

At night, they lay down with a sigh and a frown,
For although your bed looks very nice,
You sleep not a wink, but you shrivel and shrink,
Then start searching for lice.

Then morning comes round it's bitterly cold,
The carriers run out for the tea,
With a shake of the head, you run back to bed,
Yes a P.O life is no life for me.

You lie and you scoff, Yorkshire pud and ice cream,
By the round, the yard and the block.
Then suddenly find it's only a dream,
Bread's up it's near ten o'clock.

Along with the bread, you get a bit of cheese,
That wouldn't fill Mickey the Mouse,
Another shake of the head, you scoff all the bread,
Then sit down and start to de-louse.

You just settle down, when the news flashes round,
Between curses and swears made by all,
They shout and they bark, get into the park
It's time for the bloody roll call.

Like sheep in a pen, you are herded an then
They give you a search just for fun,
And you cough, and you sneeze, and you bend at the knees,
Until all the searching is done.
By Officers who, in their breeches of blue,
And arms like Al Caponi,
It's bloody near dark, when you get out of the park,
In time for your stewed macaroni.

You finish your stew, then start to brew
Some tea with wood that is knocked,
From part of your bed or Italian shed,
That Toni thought he had locked.

You may think we are well off and get plenty of scoff,
But we brew, and we eat just because we get tea for the brew,
And eat curried stew,
Thanks to the British Red Cross.

Forgotten Heroes

You have sung the well earned praises,
Of the lads who fought and fell,
Beneath the scorching Libyan sun,
On Russia's frozen Hell.

In Singapore's Great Fortress,
On Dunkirk's bloody shore,
Their names may die,
But memories will live for evermore.

But the waiting and the wondering,
Of them who fought and live,
And now are caged in prison camps,
But little thought you give.

Oh! The waiting and the wondering,
The prayers and silent tears,
For that great day, when those who may,
Will sound "The last all clear."

They fought till every gun was stopped,
Till every hound was spent,
Then with the cry "Long live the King",
With cold steel in they went.

But dauntless courage and cold steel,
Were never made for tanks,
To them I say. Who lived that day,
God bless you, many thanks.

Oh! The waiting, and the longing,
For a smile or gentle kiss,
From loved ones near and yet so far,
Whose tender care they miss.

Empires come and conquer,
And Empires disappear,
But those who fought and lived that day,
Still wait "The Last all clear."

Egypt (As it is)

Land of heat and sweaty socks,
Land of sand and tons of rocks,
Streets of sorrow, streets of fame,
Streets to which we give no name,
Arab thieves and pestering wogs,
Stinks of dirt and slinking dogs,
Blazing sand and aching feet,
Cypoe guts and Camel meat,
Clouds of choking dust that blinds,
Drives a bloke clean off his mind,
Arabs heaven, soldiers Hell,
Land of Pharaohs,
"Fare thee well."

The Letter

What little things make life's Sunny days,
Small happenings print gold into the greys,
A letter is a well loved scrawl,
A little scrap of paper, that is all it might have been,
A square of heaven indeed,
For with it's coming someone's day looked up,
And happiness ran brimming in the cup,
Eyes filled with stars, a heart began to sing,
Life's joys depend on such a little thing.

Till Death

We promised each other that cold winter's morn,
Then to bind us still closer, our baby was born,
They both have my love, my mind, and my heart,
Remember dear Maudy, till death do us part.

The Oceans divide us, my love remains firm,
I'll fight for my own till the enemy squirm,
Then homeward my ship, on it's journey will start,
As always devoted one, till death do us part.

Our small humble home once more we will share,
For I love you my darling, with a love that is rare,
No more from your side will I ever depart
As God is our judge dear, "Till death do us part."

Cross of Red

A cross of red, a simple sign,
Yet what a place it holds,
It's flag is flown o'er all the world,
All creeds it's powers enfolds.

Without it nothing could be done,
No mission could go through,
No soul could rest, no heart be strong,
Disasters would accrue.

In times of hate, and war and strife,
It carries on the same,
The more it's deeds are called upon,
The brighter glows it's flame.

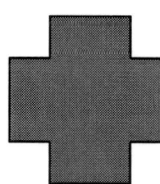

It is on the spot at every call,
It acts in night or day,
When fo¹ks are sick and things go wrong,
It gets there right away.

Sometimes we're apt to treat it light,
It's deeds are things of course,
We pass it by without a thought,
And fail its deeds to endure.

Yet most of us, when things look black,
Upon its gifts depend,
And realize that the Red Cross,
Stands out, our greatest friend.

The things then, lads, we'll vow we'll do,
When freedom we regain,
Is do our bit, how ever small,
To help the Red Cross reign.

Peace

The thunder of war had died away,
And turmoil and strife had ceased,
But thousands lay dead on the desert field,
Men who had already found peace.

Sweat, toil, and tears, blood, dust, fire and hell,
Was the price of peace, they had won,
But the worst blow fell to women at home,
Everyone was some mother's son.

The peace they found was not of the world,
Far greater and finer their share,
No more worry and trouble,
Mind and soul were at rest.

Everything was left in God's care,
Their lives they had given for land and kin,
So that loved ones may live without fear,
Thousands had died so that millions might live,
So the price of God's peace is not dear.

Parcel Day

They line up for their parcels,
All ready at the gate,
Old boxes tucked beneath their arms,
Excitement really great,
The 'Q' comes out and beckons,
They all come trooping in,
See Sgt. Majors on fatigues,
Stick holes in every tin.

Each man grabs a parcel,
And hold it to him tight,
With a smile of joy he starts to plan,
The scoff he'll have tonight,
As quick as light he lifts the lid,
To scan the fine array,
And see which butter, milk or jam,
Has luckily come his way.

They're off to the billet,
Their hungry mouths to cram,
And there starts the shouting,
"Who'll give marmalade for jam?"
Then starts the general scramble,
The mixing's at its height,
With butter, jam and lots of klim,
They stir with all their might.

Then out comes prunes and raisins,
A biscuit, jam and bread,
And all goes in the trifle,
With which they end their spread,
The tea comes up, the stage is set.
They start to scoff, they're able!
The goodly things all spread around,
Are like an Aesops fable.

Dear Wife

I always think of you sweetheart,
My wife so brave and true,
And though it's hard to be apart,
You know that I love you.

When evening comes, and day is done,
One little prayer I say,
"Oh Lord, keep my loved one safe,
And send me back one day."

I also pray, that our great love,
Will always be the same,
And when the dark clouds pass away,
That we shall meet again.

To you, dear wife, I write these words,
To show my love for you,
And that I'll be forever yours,
When these long days are through.

To My Wife

Some day when war is over,
I'll come back to thee,
When peace once more shall rule the Earth,
I'll safely cross the sea,
Thy longing eyes with joy will beam,
Thy heart with pleasure beat,
When home again, in sweet content,
I claim that vacant seat.

(By Pte. Littlewood, R.A.S.C,
captured Libya, June 1942.)

Alone

I see the sun descend behind the hill,
Enveloping the silvery clouds in cold,
Then twilight comes, and all the world is still,
Ere moon and stars their hidden charms unfold.
The woods are filled with hunting shades and light,
While birds forget their joyful day of song,
And nature slowly spreads the cloak of night,
To whom the hours of love and dreams belong.
Like some reluctant child I go to rest
Thinking of you dear heart, in foreign lands,
I pray that all our soldiers lives are blessed,
That I again in mine, may hold your hands,
And you, when evil minds admit defeat,
Return, beloved to make my life complete.

Thoughts of Home

I've travelled far from shore to shore,
Through many distant lands,
Nor do I wish to sojourn more,
Among their spacious sands.

Through all these days, one thought rings clear,
And echoes over the sea,
A thought of friends and loved ones, so dear,
Awaiting there for me.

With faith sincere, and courage strong,
In joyous hope they wait,
For strife to cease and we ere long,
To enter at their gate.

And when again those hearts unite,
May voices speak as one,
Not of vain glories in the fight,
But more of virtues won.

Loves Faith

For you dear one I'm ever yearning,
How could I ever forget you,
My thoughts like homing birds returning,
Where the heart is set.
Lead me down the path of peace,
To memory's golden door,
Away from all the din and sin and tragedy of war.

We have our love,
Life cannot cheat us of this splendid thing.
No power dishearten or defeat us,
Time will only bring-
New buds of hope, fresh flowers, of faith to bloom
in loves green bowers,
When God at last restores,
To us these lost and wasted hours.

Memories and Dreams

The evening shadows softly fall,
The Earth is tinged with dew.
And darling when the moon appears,
My thoughts return to you.
I dream of walks, thro' fields of green,
Neat shady oak and pine,
To me the grandest dream of all,
Is your sweet lips on mine.

These memories bring me happiness,
And pair too as it's store.
I pray that God will keep you dear,
In his sweet loving care,
And when I return to you my dear,
The skies will all be blue,
And love will find new happiness,
To make our dreams come true.

For You

She's pure and sweet and gentle,
As a lovely lissome flower.

She carries her head right proudly,
There's nothing can make her frown,
For she's given her heart to a soldier boy,
And he's fighting for his King and Crown.

She treasures each letter he sends her,
Each one is to her added joy,
And they're placed under her pillow,
As she prays," Please take care of my boy."

Maybe you're the boy she prays for,
Maybe yours is that treasure so fair,
If she is its well worth waiting,
And worth all the hardships you bear.

So don't moan if the whole world seems all array,
Don't grumble and keep feeling blue,
Be like her wear a smile,
Take her faith golden love your just due.

After the War is Over

After the war is over,
We will go home in clover,
Back to our towns and fun.

We'll sail the mighty ocean,
Back to the land we adore,
Back to our homes and loved ones,
To stay there for evermore.

We are leaving the empty spaces,
Leaving our comrades who fell,
Always remembering their faces,
As their lives they bravely did sell.

Freedom will reign forever,
Men will be saved from Hell,
Bells will be ringing and singing,
The world their joy to tell.

After the war is over,
After the strife is done,
We will go home in clover,
Back to our towns and fun.

Just Dreams

They've been and gone and done it Mum,
They've caught your loving son,
I went dashing into action,
And got captured by the Hun.

Now I'm sitting here and dreaming
Of how the time has flew,
Since I sat there in that easy chair,
Knocking back your Irish stew.

Just get me ready a Hotpot lass,
With custard and apple puds,
And that cup of tea you make for me,
My word won't that be good.

I'd like to see old Dad again,
And shake him by the hand,
And take him down to the "Rose and Crown",
That's one of the things I've planned.

A Tribute to the Women of England

The cottage was a thatched one,
The inside clean and neat,
As a mother sat there rocking
The cradle at her feet.

Outside the night had fallen,
And all was peace and quiet,
When suddenly the sirens,
Came wailing through the night.

People ran for shelter,
Children screamed with fear,
For one and all knew what it meant,
As the planes came roaring near.

The guns barked out their warning,
The searchlights cut the sky,
But they only served one purpose,
To keep the bombers high.

When suddenly above the roar
Of scores of Ack-Ack guns,
There came the dreaded whistling bombs,
Dropped by the callous huns.

In the cottage all was peaceful,
And at the bottom of the stairs,
Knelt that woman and her baby,
As she softly said her prayers.

And she looked towards the Heaven,
Her eyes shone full of faith,
She softly murmured "God above,
Please keep my baby safe."

He's already lost his Daddy,
For he gave his life in France,
So if I could get killed this night,
Please give my child a chance.

And though her cheeks were wet with tears,
Her voice was full of pride,
She whispered "May God bless you",
And the bombs fell outside.

And although that cottage stood
Outside the town all on its own,
A bomb crashed through the centre
Of that peaceful little home.

And when the raid was over,
And the bombers had passed by,
They searched that ruined cottage,
And heard a baby's mournful cry.

They found beneath the ruins,
That brave young soldier's wife,
But her dead and battered body,
Had saved her baby's life.

And so when you go into action,
And you maybe feel afraid,
Just think what the woman stand,
In any big air raid.

A Little Thrush

When I was a boy I caught a thrush,
And placed it in a cage
Away from it's home in a hawthorn bush,
And its mates, in a purple cage.

The little captive sadly sang
Of it's freedom that was spent,
I did not know till later years,
How much this freedom meant.

But now as I captive stay,
Far away from freedom's bush,
I think again of childhood days,
And the freedom I took from that thrush.

My Wife

You've always been so good to me,
You've helped in every way,
Your love's made life complete for me,
Much more I cannot say.

But this I know, that no-one else
Could ever be like you,
Nor could I, if I searched the world,
Find anyone so true.

The Battle for Sed-Jenane, March 2nd 1943

'Twas the rattle of machine guns,
Far into the hills, and mortar bombs bursting too
Which warned the British at Sed-Jenane,
That Germans were fast breaking through.

As the daylight deepened into chilly dusk,
The enemy paused to consider his plight,
For men need to eat and sleep sometimes,
While the guards keep watch through the African night. B

So into the village, when the night was yet young,
Came Free French and gallant reconnaissance Corps,
A terrible battle they had witnessed and fought,
Leaving comrades behind who would see home no more.

Then men with their weapons lay hidden 'neath trees
Which bordered the solitary lane,
And prepared to defend with their lives if they must,
The villages of Sed-Jenane.

Many were the lorries arriving and unloading,
Not venturing to show a light,
And down came torrential Tunisian rain,
To add to the blackness of the night.

Foresters, Durhams and Lincolns stood awaiting
The Brigade Commander's plan
For however he thought fit to manoeuvre his forces,
Affected the life of each man.

Then into the attack went the Foresters next morning,
Immediately after the Dawn,
But the enemy had chosen a superior position,
And the Foresters retired out-worn.

In the afternoon their great hearts, nothing daunted,
The Foresters attacked once again,
And the Germans once more drove us back,
In the battle for Sed-Jenane.

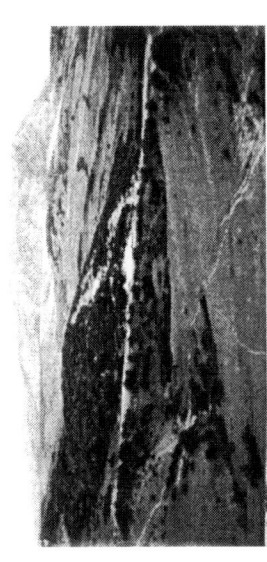

Africa

Another campaign is over, another battle won,
No more do we hear the cannon in the African sun,
But do not let this victory dazzle too much our eye,
And make us forget our comrades who now in Africa lie.

These men with whom we soldiered in blood and seat and toil,
Most stay now forever enriching African soil,
Each one a bit of England and so they shall remain,
Never to be forgotten until we meet again.

In Remembrance of my old mate, "Bless him" Jonny Kerly.

Now you have heard of a place called Tunisia,
Where a lot of fighting was done,
That's where a poor British Tommy
Was shot down by a German gun.

And raising himself on his elbows,
The blood from his wounds did flow red,
And turning around to his comrades,
There were the words that he said-

"O bury me out in the desert,
Under the Tunisian sun,
O bury me out in the desert,
My duty for England is done."

So we buried him out in the desert,
And put some stones over his grave,
We buried him out in the desert,
His life for old England he gave.

And now that we are back in Blighty,
The war is over and won,
Let us think of one left behind us, shot down by a gerry gun.

This poem refers to Captain John Alexander Kerly 2/5th Battation who was shot in the head and killed when leading a bayonet charge on a German position near Sedjenane on 2nd March 1943.

Campo Concentramento

(Song)

Now a Corporation muck cart
Overturned it's load one day,
All its rotten contents in an Itie village lay.
Now when the Ities found it,
Sure it looked so wet and damp,
They said suppose we leave it and make an Allied prison camp.

So they sprinkled it with rat traps,
Which politely they called huts,
All the roads were muddy,
And crumpled up with ruts,
They sprinkled it with fleas and lice,
And a million nits,
When they had finished it.

Now there's a place in Italy,
That everyone should know,
It's not far from Vesuvius,
Where molten larva flows.
It's very near a village on the map,
That's called Capua,
Where on a dark and stormy night,
The boys crawled through the sewer.

(Chorus)

Campo Concentramento PC 66,
Seldom you'll ever see a frown,
There's English and there's Irish,
And good old Welshmen too,
And the Scotsmen who'll never let you down.
Campo Concentramento PC 66,
There's blacks, there's whites but never blues,
And soon will come the day when we shall sail away
From Campo Concentramento PC 66.

"A Dying Soldier's Prayer."

As night descends on a lonely place,
Strange shadows play on a ghostly face,
In a dusty heap in the open air,
Lay a soldier who had fallen there.

Blood from the battle stained his hair,
As he softly utters an unheard prayer,
Sand from the desert where he had fought,
Where death and havoc had been wrought.

As he lies there a thousand thoughts
Find their passage through a tortured mind,
He thinks of home, of all things right-
A peaceful land on a summers night.

He thinks of a girl who is waiting there,
Waiting in vain for an unheard prayer,
Of rich golden fields of swaying corn,
A running stream, a shady lane.

He turns his head, chokes a cry back,
Then wipes a tear from a tired eye,
His strength is ebbing, he's sinking fast,
Fighting, and struggling to the very last.

As the sky is filled with the light of dawn,
He lies there pallid, with features drawn,
He does not stir, care or heed,
Another victim, of Hitler's vile creed.

So when you raise your glasses to your fair land,
Do not forget to toast that gallant band,
Of the fighting men of the African land,
Who risked their lives for your England

To my wife Maudey

The twentieth year is well-nigh past,
Since first our sky was overcast,
Ah! Would that this might be the last,
My wife Maudey.

Thy spirits have a fainter flow,
I see thee daily weaker grow,
It was my distress that brought thee low,
My wife Maudy.

But well thy play the housewife's part,
And all thy threads with magic art,
Have wound themselves about my heart,
My wife Maudy.

For I could see them and thee,
A sight worth seeing, I could see,
The sun would shine on them for me,
My wife Maudey.

But ah, by constant heed I know,
How oft the kindness that you show,
Transforms my smiles into a glow,
My wife Maudey.

And I know our love will last,
In the future as of the past,
To be with you is all I ask.
My wife Maudy.

(Signed with:- **"This poem is dedicated to my beloved wife. By L/Cpl. Jeffery, British Prisoner of War in Germany 1943, Dec.2**nd**."**

"My Motto"

I pass through this world but once,
Any good deed I can do, or any kindness I can show,
Let me do it now,
Let me not neglect it,
Nor defer it,
For I shall not pass this way again.

(Untitled)

Life is mostly froth and bubble,
Two things stand alone
Kindness in another's troubles
Courage in your own.

Freedom

Our heritage has always been freedom,
We cannot afford to relinquish it,
We the armed forces will
Safeguard the heritage,
If you too do your share to preserve it.

"On My Twenty Sixth Birthday."

I strove with one,
For one was worth my strife,
Nature I loved, but mostly my wife.
I'd work both hands, down to the bone,
So roll on the day when I can go home.

What I live for

I live for those that love me,
Whose hearts are kind and true,
For the Heaven that smiles above me,
And awaits my spirit too.
For all human ties that bind us,
For the task my God assigned me,
For the bright hopes left behind me,

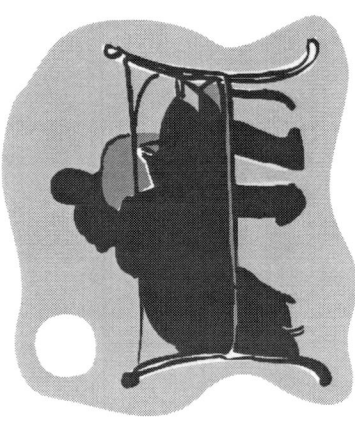

And the good that I can do.
I live for those who love me,
For those who know me true,
For the Heaven that smiles above me,
And awaits my spirits too,
For the cause that lacks assistance,
For the future in the distance,
And the good that I can do

Keep Smiling

Another New Year is here once more
What has this one for us in store?
Will I see good old England's shore?
And be home with you once more?
I've a feeling that this is true,
And hope you have the same feeling too.
Remember the saying I sent before,
Chin up, keep smiling for evermore

Future Dreams

Tho' miles of sea divide us,
I am thinking of you ever,
And yearning for the day,
When you will have to leave me never.

We'll share our dreams together,
And watch them all come true,
Oh dearest, what a paradise,
I'm so in love with you.

We'll think of years before us,
And the happiness we'll share,
Our hearts will be entwined as one,
For we will always care.

So, these are the things I'm saving,
Tho' we are far apart,
For the memory of your face so dear,
Is engraved upon my heart.

Meditation

A soldier lad was sitting on his Italian wooden bed,
The thoughts of his dear childhood days,
Were passing through his head,
As the memory took him back again to happy bygone years,
His heart was filled with happiness,
His eyes grew dim with tears;

He recalled his dear old mother with her crown of silvery grey,
His father and his brother whom he'd left so far away,
Again he seemed to listen to the rippling mountain streams,
As hand in hand he wandered with the sweetheart of his dreams.

They had always been together,
And as youngsters they had played,
Among the purple heather of that silent Scottish glade,
They had seen the narrow lanes and the weaving fields of corn,
And listen to the plovers calling in the stillness of the morn.

But his dreams had all been shattered,
When that fateful blow did fall,
When with millions of his countrymen,
Did answer Britain's call,
Since then the world's been hidden,
In a mist of blood and tears,
But he's hoping to return home to times,
Like bygone days.

(Signed with "Just for you dear wife I long," your Fred.")

Swing Song

My little lad is the image of his Dad,
You can bet your life he's his Mother's pride and joy,
I take him upstairs and watch him say his prayers,
"Please God, make me a good little boy."
I tuck him in and sing him songs my mother used to sing,
He looked at me and says now,
"I don't like that sort of thing,
O Daddy sing me to sleep with a swing song."

The Desert Rats

We may live like rats, in holes dug deep,
On the sand we eat,
On the sand we sleep,
Defending to the last,
One of Natures post,
Defying Hitler and Goering's host.

By Staff Sergeant, Eric Adams
Tobruk, 1941-42.

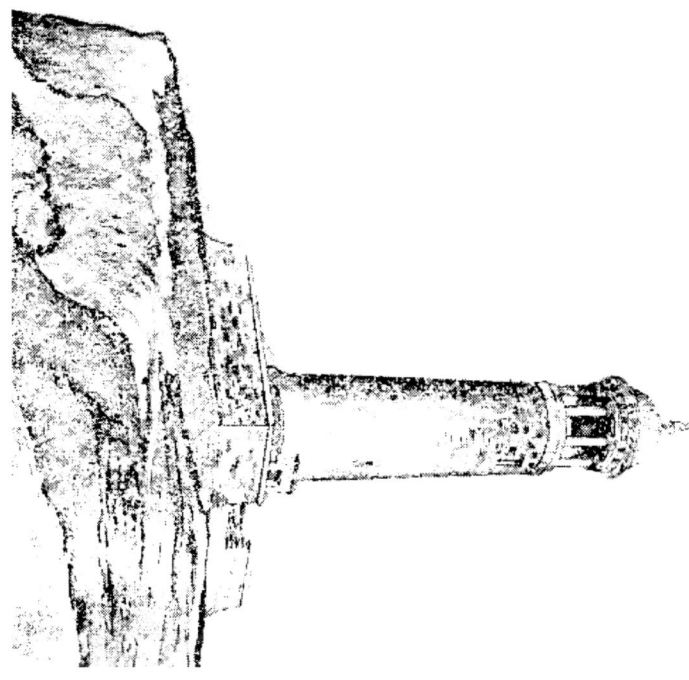

CRICH MEMORIAL

Oh, Great Majestic Cenotaph,
With your radiant light,
Shining – in memoriam
Through the darkest night.
Some people do not seem to know just what you represent,
The younger generation don't realise what war meant.

There's those who DO remember –
They come but once a year,
Some – to stand in silence,
While others shed a tear.
Then off they go, their various ways,
The wreaths of poppies laid, -
Left underneath your guiding light,
To wither and to fade.
Oh, Great and Glorious Monument,
When will they understand
That greed and war must be no more,
Let peace reign in every land.

Printed in Firm & Forester April 1982
Un-credited